Towns & Villages of Britain:
DERBYSHIRE

Roly Smith

Series editor: Terry Marsh

Published by Sigma Leisure – an imprint of
Sigma Press, 1 South Oak Lane, Wilmslow, Cheshire SK9 6AR, England.

British Library Cataloguing in Publication Data
A CIP record for this book is available from the British Library.

ISBN: 1-85058-622-5

Series Editor: Terry Marsh

Typesetting and Design by: Sigma Press, Wilmslow, Cheshire.

Cover Design: MFP Design & Print

Cover photographs: main picture – Edensor parish church, smaller pictures, from top – Town End, Taddington; Chapel-en-le-Frith; The Crescent, Buxton.

Photographs: by the author

Map: Morag Perrott

Printed by: MFP Design & Print

Foreword

Derbyshire has the best of both worlds – it is a county of wonderfully varied landscapes, and beautiful and historic villages and towns. I often think that the only thing it lacks is a coastline – but then I suppose we can't have everything.

From the dramatic moorlands and high limestone plateau of the High Peak and Derbyshire dales, which form the basis of Britain's first National Park, to the rich, farming landscapes of the south and the industrialised former coal-mining villages of coal measures to the east of the county, Derbyshire is in many ways the epitome of England.

The character of the county comes through strongly in its towns and villages, where the people who shaped the landscape have lived in many cases since Saxon times. The architecture of the buildings in Derbyshire towns and villages usually reflects its underlying geology, with gritstone gracing Dark Peak villages, limestone in the White Peak and red brick in the south and east, where stone is less abundant. Derbyshire's vernacular architecture is always sensitive to its surroundings, and we are blessed with some of the loveliest village and townscapes in Britain, many of which are now protected as conservation areas.

This priceless heritage needs to be protected carefully if we are to pass it on enhanced and unharmed to future generations. I hope that this book, which celebrates the diversity of Derbyshire towns and villages, will make us all more aware of what we have and make us even more determined to safeguard it for the future.

Cllr Martin Doughty
Leader of Derbyshire County Council and Chairman of the Peak District National Park Authority

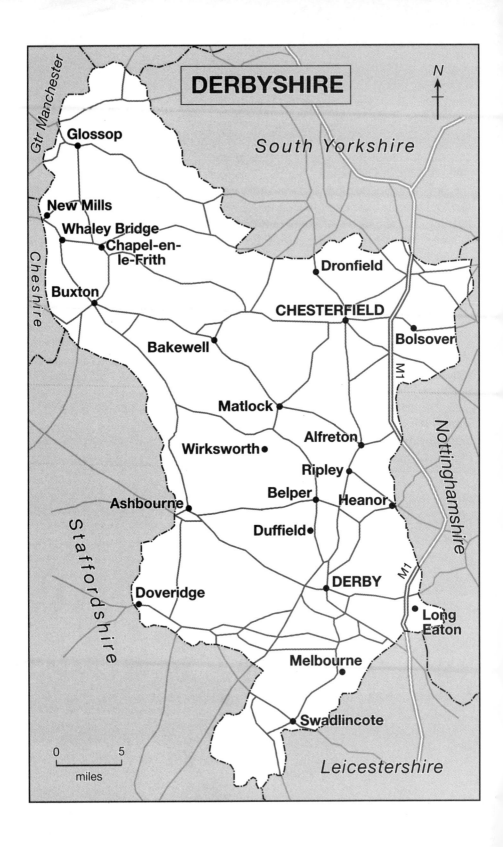

DERBYSHIRE

N

Gtr Manchester

South Yorkshire

Glossop

New Mills

Whaley Bridge

Chapel-en-le-Frith

Cheshire

Buxton

Dronfield

CHESTERFIELD

Bakewell

Bolsover

M1

Matlock

Wirksworth

Alfreton

Ripley

Nottinghamshire

Belper

Heanor

Ashbourne

Duffield

Staffordshire

Doveridge

DERBY

M1

Long Eaton

Melbourne

Swadlincote

0   5
miles

Leicestershire

Contents

Introduction

Introduction to the Series

The 'Town and Villages of Britain' is a series of titles detailing a county-by-county approach to the many delights and fascinations of our country's cities, towns, villages and hamlets. There is much of interest and value throughout our towns and villages, but not all of it is widely documented, and some of it, particularly local customs, folklore and traditions, is in danger of being lost forever. By bringing all this information together, county-by-county, it becomes possible to build a unique and substantially comprehensive library of knowledge.

All the books in the series are compiled to the same specification and in gazetteer format, and include information about the way or the reason a town or village evolved; references to anything associated with the preservation of the past, such as museums, heritage centres, historic or prehistoric sites, battle sites, places of worship and other locally or architecturally important buildings. Landscape features are also detailed, including important natural history sites, geological sites, water features, etc. as is information about important local people, and details of events or traditions, such as well-dressings and rush-bearing ceremonies. There are also notes about any significant present-day informal amenity/recreational features, like country parks, open access land, Areas of Outstanding Natural Beauty, nature reserves, and Sites of Special Scientific Interest. Finally, information is given on any significant Roman or prehistoric context, and any anecdotal or endemic folklore references associated with the town or village which might illustrate a particular way of life or social development. The books are therefore eminently suitable for anyone interested in their own locality or in local history; students of history, folklore and related subjects; professional journalists wanting up-to-date and comprehensive information; public relations and similar businesses; photographers and artists, and, of course, the tourists and visitors to the counties.

Explanatory Notes

It has been suggested that to qualify as a village, a 'community' must possess a school, a pub, a post office and a church. Such a requirement, however, excludes a large number of places in Derbyshire that are of immense interest, many having important historical associations, and which have played a vital part in the development of the county and its people. So, for the purposes of the books in this series, the criteria for inclusion have been kept deliberately simple: there must be something of interest about the place; or it must have associations with events and people of countywide or wider significance.

Often, the 'something of interest' will simply be the village church (its history, contents or architecture), or its green or a river bridge. In addition, the village may be important to the heritage of the county because it maintains the traditions, ways and beliefs of Derbyshire culture, or has played a key role in the social, economic or political history of the county or the country as a whole.

Only occasionally, however, is the village pub of special interest in this context, and often the development of large supermarkets within easy travelling distance of the villages has, sadly, signalled the demise of the traditional village shop. Local schools have often been swallowed up by larger schools, and far too many post offices are proving difficult to sustain as viable concerns. So, while that 'classic' definition of a village has much to commend it, in reality it is today too restrictive.

Quite what makes a town is another, arguable, matter. But the precise definition is here not too important; it's the place and its people, not its status, that matters. As a very broad distinction, that no-one should take seriously, a 'hamlet' (a few of which appear in these books) is a distinct community, while a 'village' could be said to be a hamlet with a church, and a 'town' is a village with a market.

In many cases, the historical development of the community, whether a tiny village, a town or a city, is fascinating in itself, and so it is that each entry gradually builds up a picture of Derbyshire that is unique. That is what this book endeavours to portray, in a logical and easily accessible way, as well as being a source of reference.

Inevitably, there will be places that have been omitted that others might argue should have been included. But the value each community has to bring to a work of this nature has been carefully weighed; invariably, borderline cases have been given the benefit of the doubt and included.

It is equally clear that, taken to its logical conclusion, this book would be ten times larger, and there has had to be a considerable degree of selective editing to make it of manageable size. One day, perhaps, there could be one book that says everything there is to say about Derbyshire. But could we afford to buy it? Could we carry it? Would we want it, when part of the beauty of what does exist is the range of voices and shades of opinion so many different authors can bring?

Following the General Introduction, the book becomes a gazetteer, listing the towns and villages of the county in alphabetical order.

After each town or village name there appears, in square brackets, [ ], the name of the relevant district council (see below).

Next appears a two-letter, four-figure grid reference, which will pinpoint the settlement to within half a mile (one kilometre). This is followed by an approximate distance from some other, usually larger, settlement, together with an equally approximate direction indicator.

Those features or people 'of interest' directly associated with the settlement are highlighted in bold text, while an index lists other features or people only incidentally associated.

Where information is given about events, such as agricultural shows, or facilities, like museums, details of dates and hours of opening are available from either the Peak District National Park, who publish an annual bulletin, or from any of the Tourist Information Centres listed below.

Local Authorities

Amber Valley Borough Council, Town Hall, Market Place, Ripley, DE5 3BY, Tel: (01773) 570222

Bolsover District Council, Sherwood Lodge, Bolsover, Chesterfield, S44 6NF, Tel: (01246) 240000

Chesterfield Borough Council, Town Hall, Chesterfield, S40 1LP, Tel: (01246) 345345

Derby City Council, Council House, Corporation Street, Derby, DE1 2FS, Tel: (01332) 293111

Derbyshire County Council, County Hall, Matlock, Derbyshire, DE4 3AG, Tel: (01629) 580000

Derbyshire Dales District Council, Town Hall, Matlock, DE4 3NN, Tel: (01629) 580580

Erewash Borough Council, Town Hall, Ilkeston, DE7 5RP, Tel: (0115) 944 0440

High Peak Borough Council, Council Offices, Hayfield Road, Chapel-en-le-Frith, Stockport, SK12 6QJ, Tel: (01663) 751751,

North East Derbyshire District Council, Council House, Saltergate, Chesterfield, S40 1LF, Tel: (01246) 231111

South Derbyshire District Council, The Civic Offices, Civic Way, Swadlincote, DE11 0AH, Tel: (01283) 22100

Tourist Information Centres

Ashbourne, 13 Market Place, Ashbourne, DE6 1EU, Tel: (01335) 343666

Bakewell, The Old Market Hall, Bridge Street, Bakewell, DE45 1DS, Tel: (01629) 813227

Buxton, The Crescent, Buxton, SK17 6BQ, Tel: (01298) 25106

Chesterfield, Peacock Information Centre, Low Pavement, Chesterfield, S40 1PB, Tel: (01246) 345777

Derby, Assembly Rooms, Market Place, Derby, DE1 3AH, Tel: (01332) 255802

Glossop, The Gatehouse, Victoria Street, Glossop, SK13 8HT, Tel: (01457) 855920

Matlock Bath, The Pavilion, Matlock Bath, DE4 3NR, Tel: (01629) 55082

Ripley, Town Hall, Market Place, Ripley, DE5 3BT, Tel: (01773) 841488

National Park Visitor Centres

For all postal and general enquiries: Peak District National Park Office, Aldern House, Baslow Road, Bakewell, DE45 1AE, Tel: (01629) 816200

Castleton, Castle Street, Castleton, Tel: (01433) 620679

Edale, Fieldhead, Edale, Tel: (01433) 670207

Fairholmes, Upper Derwent Valley, Tel: (01433) 650953

Derbyshire

'A lovely child's first alphabet..'

John Ruskin, the influential 19th-century author, critic and conservationist, was introduced to the delights of Derbyshire at an early age. His mother and father, who were already under the spell of the county, took young John to Matlock for the first time at the tender age of ten, in 1829.

His precocious talent in poetry and art was actively encouraged by his parents, and it blossomed in the Derbyshire hills. One of his first known pencil drawings is of Saxton's New Bath Hotel at Matlock Bath. Many years later he was to recall his many happy walks among the cliffs of the Matlock Gorge, expressing his gratitude to his parents for yielding to his 'subterranean passion' of cave exploration, and even admitting to being a little frightened himself when they visited the 'terrible' Speedwell Mine at Castleton.

Ruskin was later to describe Derbyshire as 'a lovely child's first alphabet; an alluring first lesson in all that is admirable; and powerful chiefly in the way it engages and fixes the attention.' There can be little doubt that it exerted a major influence on his later thinking about landscape and scenery.

He appealed to fellow learned travellers to 'think of what this little piece of mid-England has brought into so narrow a compass of all that should be most precious to you. In its very minuteness it is the most educational of all the districts of beautiful landscape known to me.'

As an adult, Ruskin was to make many journeys to Derbyshire, and in fact, nearly ended his days there. While staying at Matlock during the wet summer of 1871, he caught a chill which developed into a severe attack of 'internal inflammation', which nearly killed him.

Ruskin's concern for the Derbyshire landscape was perhaps most graphically illustrated by his famous and much-quoted outburst in Letter V of his *Fors Clavigera* against the building of the Midland Railway line through Monsal Dale in 1863.

'There was a rocky valley between Buxton and Bakewell, once upon a time, divine as the Vale of Tempe...you might have seen the Gods there morning and evening – Apollo and all the sweet Muses of the light – walking in fair procession on the lawns of it, and to and fro among the pinnacles of its crags.'

'You Enterprised a Railroad through the valley – you blasted its rocks away, heaped thousands of tons of shale into its lovely stream. The valley is gone, and the Gods with it; and now, every fool in Buxton can be at Bakewell in half an hour, and every fool in Bakewell at Buxton; which you think a lucrative process of exchange – you Fools Everywhere.'

The fact that the Monsal Dale viaduct is now the focal point of one of the most photographed views in Derbyshire, and protected as a scheduled monument on the modern Monsal Trail, in the heart of Britain's first and busiest

National Park, says something about the changing taste in scenery since Ruskin's day.

At the Crossroads of Britain
It has often been said that Derbyshire is a county of contrasts, and it is an unquestionable truism. Straddling the border between Highland and Lowland Britain, it has the best of both worlds – from the rugged and forbidding Pennine moorlands of the Dark Peak to the sweet, pastoral lowland meadows of the Lower Dove and Trent.

This accident of geography also means that in terms of natural history, the county stands at the crossroads of Britain – where southern species reach their northern limit and northern species are at the limit of their range to the south.

Examples of this are the typically northern moorland species such as the mountain hare, cloudberry and bearberry, and the southern species in the limestone dales such as the ivy-leaved bellflower and melancholy thistle, and birds such as the nuthatch.

This 'Great Divide' is also reflected in the effect that Man has had on the landscape. Towns and villages in the Peak District are often small and isolated and built, not of the red brick of the Lowlands, but of the abundant native stone. Here also there are many more stone-built reminders of the ancient past, including the many burial mounds or 'lows' which crown so many hills in the Peak District. Prehistoric monuments also remain such as the magnificent Arbor Low stone circle and henge near Parsley Hay, and the Nine Ladies stone circle on Stanton Moor.

The hedgerows and arable fields which typify the Midlands, once you have crossed the 'border' north of Ashbourne, give way to mile after mile of drystone walls criss-crossing stony pastures, where pastoral farming of sheep and cattle predominates.

There is even a recognisable change in the behaviour and manner of people. Peaklanders (the old word is 'Peakrills') are definitely from North Country stock – they are more abrupt and keep themselves to themselves, using short, blunt words compared with the long-winded and more gregarious southerners. This is also reflected in their attitude to religion. Over the northern 'border' Nonconformism – particularly Methodism – is strong, with long, moralising sermons conducted in Spartan chapels by ministers who specialise in delivering dire warnings of hellfire and damnation for the uninitiated. This is in sharp contrast to the trendy vicars and padded pews which typify the south of the county.

The Rocks Beneath
Geologically speaking, Derbyshire is divided into four quite distinct regions, which, in turn, have shaped its landscape and towns and villages. These are the southern clay and sandstone area roughly south of a line from Derby to Ashbourne; the sandy coal measures east of Derby and Chesterfield with the band of Magnesian limestone around Bolsover and Whitwell; the central limestone plateau of the White Peak between Ashbourne and Castleton; and the high Millstone grit moorlands in the north of the county, which are known as the Dark Peak.

'The Derbyshire Dome' is a geomorphological feature drilled into the memory of generations of geography students, and is still a pretty fair description.

The largely Carboniferous age rocks of the northern half of the county were laid down in semi-tropical conditions around 280-345 million years ago, when what was to become Derbyshire was several degrees south of the equator and flooded by a warm, shallow sea. This was when the enormously thick beds of limestone which are now exposed as the White Peak plateau were laid down as countless millions of tiny sea creatures died and drifted down to the sea bed. Following a series of minor volcanic interludes, the limestone was covered by beds of coarse grit and silt laid down by rivers flowing from the north. This was compressed and compacted to form the alternating layers of millstone grit and softer shales which now form the moorland areas known as the Dark Peak and the broad shale valleys below, now occupied by Derbyshire's major rivers such as the Derwent and Wye.

The whole 'sandwich' was overlaid yet again by the tropical rain forests of the Carboniferous period, which created the coal measures of the former Derbyshire-Nottinghamshire coalfield, running from Chesterfield south to Ilkeston. Smaller areas of coal measures also outcrop in the west of the county, in the Goyt Valley and west of Hayfield.

At the end of the Carboniferous period, these sedimentary rocks were subjected to enormously strong folding and faulting, followed by an uplift in the earth's crust which created that famous Derbyshire Dome and, incidentally, the rest of the Pennine anticline.

Gradual erosion and denudation, accelerated by the action of glaciers and the frost-thaw conditions of successive Ice Ages, wore down the dome from the centre, creating the now familiar upturned horseshoe of gritstone and shale, with the coal measures on either side and the older limestone exposed in the middle. It can be most easily compared to the balding pate of a man's head, the White Peak limestone forming the exposed scalp at the centre, with the shales, grits and coal measures representing the remaining 'hair' on either side and at the back.

The red-coloured sandstones and clays of the south of the county were laid down after the Carboniferous rocks to the north, in arid, semi-desert conditions during the Triassic period, 225-280 million years ago. These rocks are much softer and more susceptible to erosion and create the richer and more fertile soils of the south, over which has been deposited the considerable alluvium deposits of the Trent, Dove and Derwent.

Not surprisingly, the varied geology of the county has played a major part in the building materials and styles of the vernacular architecture of its towns and villages.

Man's Influence

As the last glaciers of the Ice Age retreated around 12,000 years ago, they left a landscape much like the tundra of northern Canada or Greenland of today. Trees, such as pine, birch, lime and ash, quickly colonised the bleak landscape and thick forests soon cloaked the dale bottoms, spreading up to cover even the highest moorlands of Kinder Scout and Bleaklow. Evidence of this extensive forest cover can still be seen in the weathered birch boles which emerge from the sides of the thick peat groughs of these now barren moors.

And it is here, in what are now perhaps the most inhospitable places in the county, that some of the first evidence of Man's presence in Derbyshire can still be found by the observant visitor. Tiny slivers of flint – known to archaeologists as microliths – can sometimes be picked up from the sides of those groughs or haggs. These minuscule fragments of imported stone were hafted onto arrows, which were discarded or lost by Mesolithic (Middle Stone Age) hunters perhaps as much as 10,000 years ago. It is a spine-chilling experience to handle them for the first time since then.

Few remains of the temporary camp sites of these first hunter-gatherers have survived, but in the caves of the White Peak dales and the Magnesian limestone gorge of Creswell Crags, on the Nottinghamshire border, even earlier traces of settlement have been found. Flint knives and scrapers used by Neanderthal Man – dating back perhaps 100,000 – 35,000 years to the Palaeolithic or Old Stone Age – have been found in the caves of Creswell Crags. The caves lay claim to being the northernmost outpost of Man dating from the time of the last Ice Age that has so far been discovered. And an inscribed portrait of a horse's head and the figure of a masked man found on scraps of bone here are thought to be among the earliest examples of true art in Britain.

Other flint tools have been excavated from caves in Miller's Dale, Lathkill Dale and Dowel Dale at the head of the Dove valley, and a beautifully fashioned, flint hand axe was found at Hopton, near Wirksworth.

The great prehistoric monuments of Derbyshire are almost exclusively found in the uplands of the Peak District, where the more pastoral farming practices have served to preserve them. Principal among these is the isolated prostrate stone circle and henge monument at Arbor Low, high on the White Peak plateau near Parsley Hay, which is sometimes dubbed 'the Stonehenge of the North' and dates from the same period as its much better-known Wiltshire counterpart.

Most remains from the Neolithic, or New Stone Age, show us not how these first permanent settlers lived, but how they died. The chambered tombs of Minninglow, near Ballidon, and Five Wells, above Taddington, show how the more important members of society were buried in stone cists – from where their bones may have been periodically removed for certain ceremonial or ritual occasions.

Moving into the Bronze Age, it is again the evidence of burial practices which tells us most in the modern landscape about how these people lived. There are estimated to be at least 500 barrows – or burial mounds – scattered across the county dating from this period. Nearly all are situated on hilltops or high points in the landscape, and paradoxically most have the suffix 'low' from the Old English 'hláw' for burial mound or hill.

It is in this period, dating from perhaps 2700 years ago, that the first real evidence of farming and settlement can be traced, mainly on the Eastern Moors of the Peak District. Here, on places like Big Moor and Gardom's Edge, systematic archaeological investigation has led to clearance cairns, field systems, hut circles and burial mounds being identified. It seems that arable fields grew crops and sizeable communities lived and thrived on these now bleak moorlands, but little evidence has been found for similar settlement elsewhere in the county, except for the early Bronze Age settlement site identified at Swarkestone.

The Iron Age (about 2000 years ago) was the age of the hill fort, and impressive examples can be found at places such as Mam Tor at the head of the Hope Valley, and Fin Cop, overlooking Monsal Dale. These huge banked and ditched enclosures were once thought to be purely military in origin, but are now believed to have more peaceful uses, perhaps as summer sheilings from where the tribe's livestock could be observed. But again, very little remains, except for isolated and random finds, to show us how these people – part of a North Country tribe known as the Brigantians – lived.

It was the abundant and easily accessible lead ore found in the limestone areas of the White Peak that first attracted the Romans into Derbyshire, in the latter part of the first century. Forts were built at Navio, near Brough in the Hope Valley, and at Melandra, near Glossop, at the entrance to Longdendale. Later, more substantial settlements were made around the warm springs at Buxton (Aquae Arnemetiae) and on the outskirts of modern Derby, where the fort of Little Chester (Derventio) has been excavated.

The great mystery of the four centuries of Roman occupation of Derbyshire is the whereabouts of the lead mining centre known as Lutudarum, whose name has been found moulded into several pigs of Roman lead which were exported all over Britain. When the Carsington Reservoir was constructed in the 1980s, an excavated site here was thought to be a possibility, but it remains unproven. Lutudarum could well be still waiting to be identified in the Matlock or Wirksworth area, at the centre of the earliest lead mining activity.

The Roman period was a largely settled one in Derbyshire, as in the rest of the country. Many small Romano-British farms, and even villas, sprang up in the county, some of which, such as the sites at Roystone Grange, near Ballidon; Chee Tor, near Blackwell; and most recently at Littlehay Grange Farm, Ockbrook, near Derby, have been excavated. There are undoubtedly many more awaiting discovery as archaeologists are now sure than the population of Roman Britain was far greater than had been previously estimated.

We now also know that the period between the Romans and the Normans – usually termed in history books as 'the Dark Ages' – was anything but dark. It saw a wonderful flowering of art and sculpture which is witnessed by Derbyshire's outstanding collection of Dark Age Saxon preaching crosses – the finest outside Northumbria. Excellent examples can be found at Bakewell, Bradbourne, Eyam, Hope and Ilam in the Peak District, while Repton's surviving Saxon crypt and chancel bear evidence to this sleepy little town's former importance as a famous Mercian monastery and the burial place of the Saxon St Wystan.

The first Anglian people who colonised the Peak District were known as the Pecsaete, or people of the Peak, while the south of the county fell under the influence of the powerful kingdom of Middle England – Mercia – which was governed from Tamworth, just across the Staffordshire border. For a period, Derbyshire and the Peak District appear to have acted as a buffer between the states of Mercia and Northumbria until Mercia finally attained ascendancy by the end of the eighth century.

Repton was the scene of a further invasion in 874 and 877 when Danish armies over-wintered there, establishing political control of eastern England under what became known as the Danelaw. It was during this time that Derby first got its name from the Old Scandinavian tongue, meaning 'place where deer are seen'. It later went back to its Saxon name of Northworthy and then reverted again to the Danish 'Derby' in the tenth century.

By this time, the Saxon kingdom of Wessex held sway over the whole of Derbyshire, under the rule of King Edward the Elder, the eldest son of Alfred the Great. According to the *Anglo Saxon Chronicles*, Edward travelled north in 920 and captured the Danish borough of Nottingham. (Derby had already fallen to his sister, Aethelflaed, in 918.) Edward then travelled north to Bakewell, where he built a fortress (a burh) in the neighbourhood.

It was here that, according to the writer of the *Chronicles*, the King of the Scots; the Vikings from York; the inhabitants of Northumbria (English and Danish, Norsemen and others); and the King of Strathclyde accepted Edward as their father and lord. Thus England and Scotland were unified for the first time. A possible site of this historic burh has recently been identified in the water-meadows of the River Wye just outside Bakewell.

Many of the preaching crosses date from this period, when Christianity first arrived in the area. It is thought that the large number of carved stones found in Bakewell church may mean that it was the site of a flourishing school of Mercian sculpture at this time.

By the time of the Norman Conquest, much of the present-day pattern of villages and towns in Derbyshire was well established, as is illustrated by the Domesday Book of 1086. Only seven churches – at Ashbourne, Bakewell, Bradbourne, Darley, Hope, Repton and Wirksworth – are mentioned as being in existence before the Conquest, and some still show signs of Saxon work today, particularly those at Bradbourne and Repton.

Much of the Derbyshire part of the Peak District was held by the king at the time of Domesday, and was part of the Royal Forest of the Peak – a 40-square-mile hunting ground preserved for royalty. The Forest was administered, along with the lead mines, from Peveril Castle at Castleton. The castle was built by William Peverel, one of the Conqueror's illegitimate sons, who also built the original stronghold at Haddon Hall, near Bakewell.

Peveril Castle, high on its almost impregnable crag between the Peak Cavern Gorge and Cave Dale, is one of the earliest stone-built keeps in the country. Built in 1175, the keep was added by Henry II, a frequent visitor to the Forest. The earliest part of the castle is the curtain wall along the northern side of the castle crag.

The planned township of Castleton, which never quite filled the area contained by its Town Ditch beneath the castle walls, was probably also the work of Henry.

But even earlier than this were the so-called motte and bailey castles of the earliest years of Norman rule. Examples of these can be seen at Pilsbury, in the upper Dove Valley, and at Bakewell, standing guard over the town bridge.

Later Norman castles and fortified manors were built at Codnor, South Wingfield, Hardwick, and Haddon, and there are fine Norman churches at Melbourne, Steetley, and Ault Hucknall, and traces of Norman work in the churches at Bakewell and Barlborough among many others.

During the Middle Ages, the wealth of Derbyshire was founded on its lead and wool, and some of the fine churches, such as the beautiful, Perpendicular, towered 'Cathedral of the Peak' at Tideswell, and All Saints at Youlgreave are founded upon those riches.

The Middle Ages also saw the growth of the large estates. The great Derbyshire families such as the Cavendishes, Dukes of Devonshire, at Bolsover, Chatsworth, and Hardwick; the Vernons, Dukes of Rutland, at Haddon and Sudbury; the Stanhopes at Elvaston; the Harpur Crewes at Calke; and the Curzons at Kedleston grew rich on the estates and their produce, building the

county's matchless heritage of stately homes and parklands.

This was also the time of the first enclosures of the large, medieval open fields from the moorland which still covered much of the upland part of the county. These large, irregular fields on the outskirts of villages contrast strongly with the narrow linear fields leading from the village crofts, which were the villagers' own strip fields. The pattern of medieval enclosure is well shown in White Peak villages such as Chelmorton, Monyash and Wardlow, where it has been 'fossilised' by the drystone walls. At other places, such as around Tissington and Ashbourne, the corrugated ridge and furrow patterns created by medieval oxen ploughing teams still stand out, especially in low light or light snow. On steeper slopes, cultivation terraces known as lynchets, still visible, show that every available piece of land had to be used to grow crops in times of hardship.

But there are many more seemingly inexplicable bumps and hollows which show up in Derbyshire meadows. These can consist of square-cut platforms and depressions, and the hollows and hillocks which spread in straight, diagonal lines across many limestone pastures. The first category show the county's rich legacy of deserted medieval villages (DMVs) – there are examples at Nether Haddon, opposite Haddon Hall; Conksbury, Smerril, Hungry Bentley and Ballidon.

The cause of these depopulations is usually not simply the Black Death, as is often cited. There were many reasons for such large-scale abandonment, including most commonly the desire of the landowner to introduce more profitable sheep grazing or cropping, his need to 'improve the view' from his great house, the failure of a site for geographical reasons, and disease or pestilence.

The linear bumps and hollows on the limestone plateau are evidence of the work of 't'owd man' – the local name for former generations of lead miners. Lead mining was an important industry in the White Peak for well over 1000 years, starting with the Romans and ending in the 1870s, when cheaper imports became available. There are estimated to be about 30,000 abandoned workings in the area. The best preserved of these is the Magpie Mine, near Sheldon, which was worked more or less continuously for 200 years. It is now used as a field study centre by the Peak District Mines Historical Society.

Peak District lead miners were usually farmers as well, and this dual economy was the mainstay of the local economy for centuries, bequeathing a rich legacy in the language and landscape.

One of the greatest problems facing the lead miner was water flooding the lower reaches of the mines, and enormous sums were spent on 'de-watering' mines by underground drainage channels known as soughs.

Ironically, it was the power of the Derbyshire rivers – particularly the Derwent – which attracted the first real industrialists to the county. Foremost among these were John Lombe and George Sorocold, who established Derby's Silk Mill in 1718; and Richard Arkwright, who built the first successful water-powered cotton mill at Cromford in 1771. He also built the first

'model village' for his workers nearby, and other cotton mills at Cressbrook, Bakewell and elsewhere. Cromford could well be described as one of the birthplaces of the Industrial Revolution. It was here that Arkwright first pioneered the ideas of mass production. Indeed, if it were not for poor communications due to its isolation in the Derbyshire hills, Cromford may have rivalled Manchester or Leeds as an industrial centre. Downstream, Jedediah Strutt's cotton mill at Belper was founded a few years later in 1776, and he later developed a calico and tape mill in Derby.

The presence of ready supplies of coal, from the North Derbyshire (part of the Lancashire), Leicestershire and South Derbyshire, and Yorkshire, Nottinghamshire and Derbyshire coalfields, all on the east of the county, made Derbyshire one of the biggest sources of power in the late 19th and early 20th centuries. By 1910, there were estimated to be over 175 coal mines in Derbyshire, and 52,000 people were employed in them. Output was more than 16.5 million tons in 1906, and the proximity of ironstone and limestone placed the county in an ideal position for iron and steel production.

All this industrialisation proved the need for better communications, and Derbyshire can also lay claim to being the birthplace of the founder of the canal system. James Brindley, a largely illiterate millwright was born at Tunstead, near Buxton, in 1716. A brilliant, self-taught civil engineer, he went on to build the world's first canal for the Duke of Bridgewater in 1759, as well as the Trent and Mersey or Grand

Trunk Canal and the Oxford Canal among many others.

The building of the Derby Canal by Benjamin Outram in 1796 proved to be a key element in turning a prosperous market town into a leading centre of industry.

The famous Derby porcelain factory had been established by William Duesbury around 1750, and, helped by local supplies of coal, an iron-founding industry followed. The same Benjamin Outram who built the Derby Canal had, with Francis Beresford, founded the famous Butterley Iron Works in 1790. He was also joint promoter, with Richard Arkwright, of the Cromford Canal, which was designed to link Arkwright's mills at Cromford to the River Trent and the Midlands.

The Cromford Canal was built by William Jessop, but it was his son who heralded the coming of the Railway Age by the design and construction of the Cromford and High Peak Railway in 1830. The railway travelled 33 miles across the 1000-foot White Peak plateau. First designed as a waggonway (the stations were called 'wharfs'), it was to link the Cromford Canal with the High Peak Canal at Whaley Bridge by the ingenious use of steam-operated continuous chain inclines.

Other railways followed, including George Stephenson's Derby to Leeds line through the Derwent Valley. By 1840, no less than three railway companies were operating lines to Derby, from Nottingham, Leeds and Birmingham respectively. Within five years they had amalgamated to form the Midland Railway, and benefiting from its central position on the east coast line, Derby became a major railway centre and terminus. The Midland Railway established its locomotive and carriage works there soon after its formation, and more foundries soon followed in the town to provide other components for the burgeoning railways.

It was the construction of the Midland Line in 1863, providing the lucrative link between London and Manchester through the Wye Valley and the hills of the Peak District, which had attracted John Ruskin's wrath. But it was an amazing feat of Victorian civil engineering, and is now followed by the Monsal Trail, although there are long-term plans for its eventual reopening for passenger traffic.

Other important railways which opened up the hills and dales of Derbyshire were the Great Central Line from Sheffield to Glossop through the infamous Woodhead tunnels and Longdendale, which was built in 1847 and is now the Longdendale Trail. and the Hope Valley line, built in 1894 to link Sheffield and Stockport through Edale and still open mainly as a ramblers' route.

The industrial towns such as Derby and Chesterfield expanded rapidly during the 19th century, and by the time it was awarded city status a hundred years later in 1977, Derby had become one of the major industrial and engineering centres of the Midlands.

But in the smaller towns and villages of Derbyshire, a distinctive vernacular architecture had developed, usually based, as explained earlier, on the underlying geology of the area. Thus in the limestone area of the White Peak, cottages are built of limestone rubble, usually with more regular gritstone quoins and window surrounds. Like the warm, brown gritstone town houses of the larger villages like Bakewell and Matlock, these older houses are often roofed in gritstone slabs, which have sometimes latterly been replaced by blue Welsh slate. Out in the country, the barns and farm buildings also reflect the available building stone, which is repeated in the endless miles of dry-stone walls of the Peak. Its absence is also demonstrated in the hawthorn hedgerows of the stoneless south and east.

In the former coalfield towns and villages of the east of the county and in the clay vales to the south of Ashbourne, Midland red brick is the most common building material. In the larger industrial towns served by railways, such as Derby, Chesterfield, Belper and Ilkeston, blue engineering bricks are often employed on larger industrial buildings and Victorian civic pride is reflected in grandiose town halls.

Derbyshire today is perhaps best known for the Peak District National Park, the first to be designated in Britain, in 1951, in recognition of its outstanding and largely unspoilt scenery. It covers 555 square miles of the north of the county, taking in the limestone plateau and dales of the White Peak, and the brooding gritstone moors and edges of the Dark Peak. Over twenty-two million day visits are made to the National Park every year, making it the second-most visited National Park in the world.

But those visitors who only flock to the hills and dales of the Peak are missing a lot of what Derbyshire has to offer. It is, indeed, a county of contrasts, and the south and east of the county have a rich heritage of stately homes, wide parklands, spacious views and charming towns and villages.

Derbyshire is, as Ruskin first described it over a century ago, 'a lovely child's alphabet,' and a place where much can be learned about the heart and soul of Middle England. Writing to his friend, the Irish poet Thomas Moore, Lord Byron enquired if he had ever been to Dovedale. 'I assure you,' he told him, 'there are things in Derbyshire as noble as in Greece or Switzerland.' Derbyshire may not have an Acropolis or a Matterhorn, but in places like Arbor Low and Kinder Scout it has equivalents every bit as ancient and challenging. Derbyshire's charm, as Ruskin observed, is in its minuteness and detail, and it shows itself on a scale which is both intimate and attainable to every discerning visitor.

The Towns and Villages

ABNEY (Derbyshire Dales)

SK1979: 2 miles (3km) SW of Hathersage

Abney and its associated hamlet of Abney Grange are isolated settlements which guard the upper reaches of the Highlow Brook on Abney Moor, high above and south of the Hope Valley. First recorded as Habenai in the Domesday Book, Abney was then owned by William Peverel, the allegedly bastard son of the Conqueror, who built nearby **Peveril Castle** at Castleton.

One of Abney's most famous sons was William Newton, the so-called 'Minstrel of the Peak', who was born here in 1750. A carpenter by trade, Newton became an accomplished poet.

High on the gritstone moors, Abney was well placed to become a lead smelting centre in the 18th and 19th centuries, the lead being brought from the limestone plateau to the south. The frequent strong winds experienced here created the draught needed for smelting the ore. Abney is now a favoured centre for walkers, with the gliders of the Derbyshire and Lancashire Gliding Club occupying the ridge end at Camphill, overlooking Bradwell Dale.

Highlow Hall, to the east, is a fine, battlemented, 16th-century manor house built by the Eyre family, with a ball-topped gateway and stone dovecote. The Eyres had been important local landowners since Norman times.

ALDERWASLEY (Amber Valley)

SK3153: 2 miles (3km) E of Wirksworth

Pronounced 'Allersley', Alderwasley is a straggling, linear village which stands high overlooking the valley of

The Old Grammar School, Ashbourne

the River Derwent to the east of Wirksworth. Its main points of interest are its fine, seven-bay Georgian **hall**, originally the seat of the Hurt family, and the Victorian **parish church of St Margaret**, which stands in the grounds of the hall.

ALFRETON (Amber Valley)

SK4155: 3 miles (5km) N of Ripley

Alfreton is one of the more attractive East Derbyshire former coal mining towns, standing close to the Nottinghamshire border. Coal has been mined here since Chaucer's day, but there is nothing left now of this once great industry which gave the town its wealth and prosperity for so long.

Thankfully bypassed by the A38, Alfreton stands on a hill with an attractive High Street which broadens at the top. One of the best of its buildings of note is the fine George Hotel, which dates from the Georgian period and looks down the length of the High Street. There are a number of other 18th-century, stone-built houses in the vicinity.

The High Street leads to the large **parish church of St Martin**, with its fine Perpendicular west tower rising from a 13th-century ground floor. The nave, which contains some fine monuments, especially to the local Morewood family, has 14th-century piers and a splendid clerestory.

West of the church stands **Alfreton Hall** (private), built by the Morewoods around 1730, but with 19th-century additions. The original seven-bay house had large rusticated pilasters and an early 19th-century, four-columned Ionic porch. Alfreton Hall is now the centrepiece of a public park.

ALPORT (Derbyshire Dales)

SK2164: 3 miles (5km) S of Bakewell

Many people's candidate for one of Derbyshire's prettiest villages, Alport stands at the confluence of the Lathkill and Bradford Rivers, just south of Bakewell on the road to Youlgreave. It is a lovely little hamlet of mainly 17th- and 18th-century houses with beautiful gardens, clustered along the banks of the Lathkill, which cascades down through the village in a series of weirs to meet the Bradford coming down from Youlgreave.

This was lead mining country in the 18th and 19th centuries, and the wealth won from the lead is reflected in the quality of some of the fine old houses, and the graceful, 18th-century bridge.

The **Hillcarr Sough**, started in 1766, was the longest sough – an underground drainage canal used to take water from the lead mines – in Derbyshire. It ran for $4\frac{1}{2}$ miles from Alport to the River Derwent at Rowsley, and cost £32,000 by the time it was finished in 1787. Such were the profits being made from lead mining in those days, the sough is said to have paid for itself within two years.

Of Alport's many fine houses, **Monk's Hall** (private) is one of the best. It dates from the late 16th or early 17th century, but probably originally connected to a monastic grange. Nearby is **Harthill Hall Farm**, a gabled, 17th-century yeoman's farmhouse with stone mullioned and transomed windows.

ALSOP-EN-LE-DALE (Derbyshire Dales)

SK1655: 5 miles (8km) N of Ashbourne

The former station on the Ashbourne-Buxton line which served the tiny hamlet is now a car park on the Tissington Trail, just off the A515 north of Ashbourne. The quiet, peaceful little hamlet itself is on a narrow lane east of the main road towards Parwich, just a mile from Dovedale.

Alsop-en-le-Dale's **parish church of St Michael** is originally of Norman construction, but was substantially rebuilt by the Victorians. The nave retains its Norman features, with impressive double zigzag mouldings in the arches, but the west tower is imitation Norman, dating from 1883. An unusual feature is the extraordinary, 19th-century, square, mock-Gothic pulpit, which rather dominates the small church.

Opposite is the tall, slender, early 17th-century building known as **Alsop Hall** (private), which is built in a pre-classical style with stone-mullioned windows.

Alsop is a fine centre for exploring the White Peak, and is particularly convenient for Dovedale, with the famous **Viator's Bridge** at Milldale only a mile (1.6km) to the west.

This was the scene, in Izaak Walton's classic fisherman's tale *The Compleat Angler* (1653), where 'Viator' complains to 'Piscator' about the size of the tiny, two-arched packhorse bridge, '..why a mouse can hardly go over it: 'Tis not two fingers broad.'

AMBERGATE (Amber Valley)

SK3451: 6 miles (10km) S of Matlock

Situated where the River Amber joins the mighty Derwent, Ambergate is one of the main gateways to the Peak District for travellers going north on the A6. A fine bridge crosses the Derwent, and the village itself is surrounded by billowing deciduous woodland, including the wonderful Shining Cliff Woods, an important refuge for wildlife. The railway, road and canal are all sandwiched into the tight river valley at Ambergate, and the railway station, standing 100ft (30m) above the road, was one of the few triangular stations in Britain.

The Victorian mock-Gothic **parish church of St Anne** was built in 1891, gifted by the Johnson family of the Ambergate Wire Works, now Richard Johnson and Nephew.

ASHBOURNE (Derbyshire Dales)

SK1846: 13 miles (21km) NW of Derby

The sign at the entrance to Ashbourne says that it is the gateway to Dovedale. But Ashbourne is much more than that. It is one of Derbyshire's finest old towns in its own right, a feast of wonderful Georgian architecture. It has in **St Oswald's Parish Church** one of the most impressive and elegant churches in the country.

It was the Victorian novelist **George Eliot** (1819-80) – who based part of her novel *Adam Bede* in this part of 'Stonyshire' (Derbyshire) – who famously described St Oswald's as 'the finest mere parish church in England'. For

James Boswell, a regular visitor to the town with his friend Dr Samuel Johnson of Lichfield, the church was 'one of the largest and most luminous that I have seen in any town of the same size'.

St Oswald's is certainly one of the glories of Ashbourne. It stands on the site of a minster church which was mentioned in the Domesday Book (where Ashbourne is Esseburn or 'ash tree stream'), but most of the present building dates from its rebuilding in the 13th century. There is a dedication brass of 1241 in the south transept. The main part of the building still retains this classic Early English style, seen especially well in the south doorway with its ribbed moulding and dog-tooth decoration. Unusually for a parish church, St Oswald's has chapels to its transepts, which all adds to the spacious feeling, more typical of a small cathedral than Eliot's 'mere parish church'.

The alabaster monuments and tombs to the Cockane and Bradbourne families in the north transept chapel are justly famous, but perhaps the best known monument in Ashbourne's wonderful church is that to **Penelope Boothby**, who died in 1791 at the tender age of five. Thomas Banks's white Carrara marble figure of the sleeping child is so lifelike that she still appears to be only sleeping. Her touching epitaph reads: 'She was in form and intellect most exquisite; The unfortunate parents ventured their all on this frail bark, and the wreck was total.' Allegedly, little Penelope's parents separated at the child's grave and never spoke again.

The tower and elegant 212-foot (30m) spire of the church are in the Perpendicular style and were raised between 1330 and 50, at the crossing of the nave and transepts.

Across Church Street from St Oswald's is the magnificent, stone-built **Old Grammar School**, which was founded in 1585 by Sir Thomas Cockayne on behalf of Elizabeth I. Completed in 1610, the long array of mullioned windows faces the street beneath steeply roofed gables. Opposite the Grammar School is the classical Georgian front of **The Mansion**, built in 1685 for Dr John Taylor, another friend of Samuel Johnson, who was a regular visitor. In 1764, an octagonal, domed drawing room was added to the old house and the new façade of brick was built facing the street. Next to The Mansion are two of the many almshouses which were established in Ashbourne during the 17th and 18th centuries.

Further down St John Street is the rare sight of a 'gallows' inn sign. It crosses the street and advertises two former coaching inns – the **Green Man** and the **Black's Head** – now combined into one. St John Street leads up to Ashbourne's sloping, triangular Market Place, where weekly markets have been held since 1296 and now take place every Saturday. Ashbourne's market was first recorded in 1257, twenty-four years before the town became a borough. In 1745, on his fateful march on London which was to end at Derby, Prince Charles Edward Stuart – 'Bonnie Prince Charlie' – declared his father to be King James III in Ashbourne's Market Place.

Ashbourne's most famous tradition is the Shrove Tuesday and Ash Wednesday Football Game. This is played through the streets of the town by teams of no set number who represent the 'Up'ards' and the 'Down'ards' respectively – the Henmore Brook being the dividing line. Anything goes in this rough-and-tumble game which is thought to accurately reflect the beginnings of the game of football. The object of the game is for the Up'ards to score a 'goal' at the wall of Sturston Mill, a mile and a half upstream, or the Down'ards at a stone marking the site of Clifton Mill, a mile and a half in the opposite direction.

ASHFORD-IN-THE-WATER (Derbyshire Dales)

SK1969: 1 mile (2km) NW of Bakewell

Not exactly in the water, but certainly on the River Wye, Ashford is another candidate for Derbyshire's prettiest village. It is perhaps most famous for its six beautifully executed well-dressings, which are held annually in early June.

The medieval **Sheepwash Bridge** crosses the Wye, its low arches framed by overhanging willows. It is one of three village bridges, and a favourite subject for artists. The small enclosure to one side gives away the name, and it is still occasionally used for its original purpose. Large crowds gather to witness sheep being unceremoniously tossed into the river in order to cleanse their fleeces before shearing.

Sheepwash Bridge is close to the grey limestone **parish church of the Holy Trinity**, which was largely rebuilt in 1870, but retains the base of a 13th-century tower. It also has a Norman tympanum from the original church, complete with Tree of Life, lion and hog, over the south door. Inside the church are some fine examples of Ashford's most famous product, the so-called **Black Marble**, which was really a highly polished grey limestone

Sheepwash Bridge, Ashford-in-the Water

won from quarries and mines near the village. This attractive stone became very popular in Victorian times, and was exported all over the world. Hanging from the roof of Ashford's church are the remains of four 'virgin's crants,' paper garlands which were carried at the funerals of unmarried village girls.

The rest of the village has a pleasant range of mainly 18th-century cottages, and a former tithe barn, which now serves as an art gallery.

ASHOVER (North East Derbyshire)

SK3463: 4 miles (6km) NE of Matlock

Viewed from the rocky ridge known as The Fabric (apparently so-named because it provided the 'fabric' for much local building stone) and with the upstanding monolith of Cocking Tor in the foreground, the prospect of Ashover from the south shows a scattered village filling the pleasantly wooded valley of the River Amber. One writer has described it as 'the valley of silence and wild flowers'.

At the centre of the village is the 15th-century **church of All Saints**. One of its great treasures, apart from the Decorated-style windows, tower and spire, is the Norman font made from the abundant local lead. Described by Pevsner as 'the most important Norman font in the county', it is, oddly, the only lead font in this lead-rich district. Of the many monuments in the church, especially impressive is the alabaster tomb chest of Sir Thomas Babington, an important local landowner who died in 1518, and his wife. It has been called 'the best in Derbyshire'. There are also

brasses to James Rolleston (1507) and his wife and children, and a brass to a priest, which dates from 1510.

Next to the church is the **Crispin Inn**, which claims to date from 1416, but is more likely to date from the 17th century, as do most of the other houses in the village. The name of the inn reflects one of Ashover's traditional trades: St Crispin is the patron saint of shoemakers and cobblers.

ASTON-ON-TRENT (South Derbyshire)

SK4129: 6 miles (10km) SE of Derby

Aston stands on the River Trent and it marks the border between Derbyshire and Leicestershire, six miles south-east of Derby. The mainly Norman **church of All Saints** has parts of a Saxon cross with beautifully interlaced carving built into the outer wall of the south aisle. The base of the buttressed west tower is original Norman, with Perpendicular pinnacles rising above.

Inside the church, there is an octagonal 13th-century font, and a fine, early 15th-century, alabaster tomb chest of a man and his wife, touchingly holding hands as they have for 500 years.

Aston Hall dates from 1735 and was originally a fine Georgian mansion of five bays with central Venetian windows. It has been much enlarged over the years.

AULT HUCKNALL (Bolsover)

SK4665: 6 miles (10km) E of Chesterfield

The strange name of the village probably means 'Hucca's high nook of land', and this pleasant place, standing high above and apart from the industrial north-east of Derbyshire, is a real gem. Situated on a back lane, the low, embattled **church of St John the Baptist** is one of the finest in Derbyshire. It overlooks Hardwick Hall's beautiful parklands, with the square towers of Bess of Hardwick's great house in the distance. The battlemented Perpendicular exterior of the church does not prepare the visitor for the dark and mysterious interior, which shows the church's much earlier ancestry. The north arcade and nave are Norman, as are the narrow arches which hold up the rare crossing tower, and there is more Norman work in the plain capitals of the north arcade.

Among several interesting tombs in the church is the large, elaborate wall monument just below the east window to Anne, the first Countess of Devonshire, which dates from 1627. On the floor in front is a simple black slab which commemorates the philosopher Thomas Hobbes (1588-1679), an honoured retainer of the Cavendish family. Hobbes, author of *The Leviathan* and *De Mirabilibus Pecci: Concerning the Wonders of the Peak* – one of the first accounts of the Seven Wonders of the Peak – died at Hardwick. He was one of the leading philosophers of his day. In the north aisle is a more homely tablet which commemorates Robert Hackett, a keeper of Hardwick Park, who died in 1703. It reads:

'Long had he chas'd
The red and fallow deer,
But death's cold dart
At last has fix'd him here.'

Hardwick Hall (National Trust) 'more glass than wall' is one of Derbyshire's Big Three stately homes, ranking alongside Chatsworth and Haddon as glorious monuments to the great land-owning families who did so much to shape the history of the county. It is forever associated with the immensely powerful Tudor matriarch, **Bess of Hardwick**, and the imposing building still carries her monogram 'ES' (for Elizabeth Shrewsbury) on its six great towers. Bess was born here in 1520 and began the building of the house in 1590, towards the end of her life, after her fourth lucrative marriage to George Talbot, sixth Earl of Shrewsbury. It is a monument to her wealth and good taste, and especially famous for its magnificent tapestries and needlework, friezes and carved fireplaces, which are generally regarded as among the finest in Britain. More recently, the gardens, including an aromatic herb garden, have been restored behind their walled courtyards. The parkland, which overlooks the valley of the Doe Lea and the M1, is populated by a magnificent herd of Longhorn cattle among the stag-headed oaks. The ruins of **Hardwick Old Hall** (English Heritage) stand in the grounds, and are the interesting remains of Bess's previous Tudor mansion.

BAKEWELL
(Derbyshire Dales)

SK2168: 12 miles (19km) NW of Matlock

This little stone-built town on the banks of the River Wye commands a beautiful setting among well-wooded hills. Although it has a population of only 4000 people, it is the largest town and is generally acknowledged to be

Bakewell Parish Church

the capital of the Peak District National Park.

Bakewell – the Old English name means 'Badeca's spring', or 'well' and refers to the warm, iron-bearing springs which rise in and around the town – was founded in Saxon times, as the ancient preaching crosses and stonework in the **parish church of All Saints** testify. The Saxon foundation of the town is proven by its mention in the Domesday Book, when it was one of the few places in Derbyshire to record two priests and a church. The two Saxon crosses which now stand, blackened and weathered, in the hilltop churchyard came from outlying parts of the parish, where they were used as preaching crosses. Both date from the early ninth century, as do some of the many fragments now col-

lected in the south porch of the church. Bakewell is thought to have been the site of a local school of Saxon carvers. Later, during Norman times, a small motte and bailey castle was built just across the town bridge to guard the crossing.

The present church suffered from an over-zealous rebuilding in 1841-52. Included in this was the unusual octagonal tower and spire which now form such an important feature in views of the town. The west front of the church is, however, still essentially Norman. Inside, the west end of the nave arches and the first bay of the arcades between the nave and the aisles are also of that date. Most of the eastern end of the church, the south transept and the chancel date from the 13th century. The very decorative font dates from the early 14th century, as do the chancel stalls, which have interesting misericords.

Foremost among Bakewell church's interesting collection of monuments are those in the Vernon Chapel in the south aisle. They include ones to 'The King of the Peak', Sir George Vernon of Haddon Hall, who died in 1567, and to Sir John Manners, who died in 1584, and his wife, a rather plain-faced Dorothy Vernon. The latter two were the subject of one of the great romantic legends of the Peak. Most interesting and unusual, however, are the waist-high, upright portrait-sculptures of Sir Geoffrey Foljambe, who died in 1377, and his wife, on a wall on the south side of the nave.

Bakewell is probably best known for its culinary delicacy – the **Bakewell pudding** (never, incidentally, call them 'tarts' in Bakewell – a Bakewell pudding is quite different). The result of a mistake by the cook at the Rutland Arms, a fine Georgian building dating from 1804 in the centre of the town, Bakewell puddings became a real hit with customers. They are now exported all over the world by the three shops which claim to hold the original (secret) recipe. No visit to Bakewell is complete without the obligatory Bakewell pudding.

From the Rutland Arms, Bridge Street runs down to the fine, 14th-century town bridge over the Wye, passing on the right the **Old Market Hall.** This attractive, old, gabled building dates from the late 17th century, and now serves as a National Park and Tourist Information Centre. Behind the Market Hall is the recently completed (1998) Market Square, where the street market is held every Monday, as it has been for over 600 years. Across the River Wye stands the enormous, new, £6.3 million **Agricultural and Business Centre**, where the livestock market takes place on market days. This controversial new building with its tent-like roof structures adjoins the site of the annual **Bakewell Agricultural Show.** This takes place in July and is the biggest and most important in the Peak District. **Bakewell's well-dressings** are held at the end of July each year.

Other important buildings in the town include the **Old House**, in Cunningham Place, above and behind the church, which is now the home of the excellent Bakewell Historical Society's mu-seum. This is thought to be the oldest house in Bakewell, and dates back to early Tudor times. It was once used by employees of Richard Arkwright's mill in the town.

Jacobean **Holme Hall**, facing the water-meadows of the Wye to the north of the town, dates from 1626, and con-sists of three bays with a central projec-tion. Near here at Lumford, where Richard Arkwright had his mill, is a fine example of a low-parapeted pack-horse bridge across the Wye, dating from 1664.

A mile down the Matlock Road, sur-rounded by trees and standing on a bluff overlooking the River Wye, is ro-mantic **Haddon Hall**, one of the finest medieval mansions in Britain. Haddon was memorably described by Nikolaus Pevsner as, 'The English castle par ex-cellence, not the forbidding fortress on an unassailable crag, but the large, rambling, safe, grey, loveable house of knights and their ladies, the unreason-able dream-castle of those who think of the Middle Ages as a time of chivalry and valour and noble feelings. None other in England is so complete and convincing.'

It is the Derbyshire home of the Duke of Rutland, and owes its marvellous state of preservation to the fact that it stood empty and neglected for nearly 300 years after 1640, when the family chose Belvoir Castle in Leicestershire as their main home. This meant that the house stood frozen in time from the mid-17th century, although there are examples of work from every century from the 12th in the rambling old build-ing.

Such is their medieval perfection, Haddon's embattled courtyard and rose-entwined walls have become a common backdrop to many film and television dramas, and it continues to be a popular film set. Visitors enjoy the Chapel, still adorned with medieval wall paintings and the oldest part of the house; the Kitchens, with their time-worn oak tables and dole cupboards; the oak-panelled and galleried Great Hall; and the magnificent Long Gallery, decorated with boars' heads (Vernon) and peacocks (Manners) in the panelling. It was from here that Dorothy Vernon is claimed to have eloped with John Manners during a ball, but there is no historical truth in this romance. It was invented by the Victorians, and neither the steps nor the pretty little packhorse bridge across the Wye she is supposed to have used were there in her time. The gardens of Haddon Hall are justly famous, and in summer are a riot of roses and other traditional English flowers.

BALLIDON (Derbyshire Dales)

SK2054: 5 miles (8km) N of Ashbourne

Overshadowed by its gigantic limestone quarry, the tiny hamlet of Ballidon is, in fact, what remains of a shrunken medieval village – as the numerous earthworks, lynchets and evidence of ridge and furrow cultivation in its fields show. The tiny **chapel of All Saints** still remains, isolated in a field and surrounded by the former crofts and tofts of the shrunken village. Originally Norman in construction, the chapel (which is locked) has been much restored over the years.

At the end of the minor road which passes through the quarry is **Roystone Grange**, the site of a monastic farm which has been systematically investigated by Sheffield University over many years to reveal a continuous occupation going back to Roman and prehistoric times. The Roystone Grange Archaeological Trail interprets the finds via an easy, four-mile walk. Nearby, across the High Peak Trail, is the Neolithic **Minninglow chambered tomb**, one of the highest in the country, standing within its halo of windswept beeches (no access).

BAMFORD (High Peak)

SK2083: 4 miles (6km) E of Castleton

Bamford stands at the heart of the Dark Peak, below Bamford Edge and close to the Ladybower Reservoir and Upper Derwent Valley Dams. When the Howden and Derwent Dams were built in the early years of the 20th century, the valley of the Upper Derwent was flooded and many farms submerged under the rising waters. The 1000 or so navvies and their families were housed at Birchinlee, a temporary village of corrugated iron shacks which was known to locals as 'Tin Town'. During the Second World War, the third and largest reservoir, the Ladybower, was built, involving the inundation of the two villages of Derwent and Ashopton. The dead from the church at Derwent were reinterred in the churchyard of **St John the Baptist**, Bamford, and the living rehoused in the purpose-built hamlet of Yorkshire Bridge, below the embankment of the Ladybower Dam. There is a visitor centre which tells the story of the 'drowned villages' and the rest of the valley at Fairholmes in the

Upper Derwent Valley, below the wall of the Derwent Dam.

Bamford's elegant spired church was designed by the famous church architect William Butterfield in 1861. **Bamford Mill**, just across the road, by the river, was built as a cotton mill in 1820 and later made electrical furnaces. More recently, it has been converted to high-class accommodation units. Bamford is the home of one of the most famous of the **Peak District sheepdog trials**, held annually on Spring Bank Holiday Monday.

BARLBOROUGH (Bolsover)

SK4777: 7 miles (11km) E of Chesterfield

Barlborough is somewhat diminished by the roar of the M1, which passes only 400yds/m away, and the roundabout junction of the A616 and A619, which is even closer to the village. Standing on the Yorkshire/Derbyshire border, the village has some fine, old, stone houses with pantile roofs, but there is much new development, especially around Barlborough Links.

The **parish church of St James** was heavily restored in 1899, but there is still some medieval work to be seen, particularly the four-bay north arcade which dates from the early years of the 13th century.

Barlborough Hall (private) stands at the end of an avenue of limes to the north of the village and is one of Derbyshire's finest unspoilt Elizabethan mansions, dating from 1584. It was built for Lord Justice Francis Rodes to a design attributed to Robert Smythson, and stands alongside the better-known Hardwick Hall to the south in terms of its architectural importance.

BARLOW (North East Derbyshire)

SK3474: 4 miles (6km) NW of Chesterfield

Standing amid the small dairy and mixed farms of north-east Derbyshire on the hills to the west above Chesterfield, Barlow is perhaps best known for its annual **well-dressings**, which take place in August. The village is mentioned in the Domesday Book, and was the home of Robert Barlow, the first of Bess of Hardwick's four husbands. He died aged 14 in 1532 and was buried in the charming, small and originally Norman **parish church of St Laurence**. There are still traces of that earliest church to be seen, especially the doorways in the nave and chancel, but the church suffered from a somewhat over-exuberant Victorian restoration in 1867. Other monuments in the church include an alabaster tomb slab to Robert Barley and his wife (1467) in the Lady Chapel. The village was originally known as Barley, and the family took their name from it, later changing it to Barlow.

West of the village stands **Woodseats Hall** (private), the 16th/17th-century home of the Mower family. Arthur Mower was the agent to the Barley family in the 16th century, and kept a remarkable diary from 1555 to 1610, the fifty-two volumes of which are now kept in the British Museum. He recorded the death of Bess of Hardwick in 1608 and recalled her as 'a great purchaser and getter together of much goods' and mentioned that she 'builded Chattesworth, Hardwick and Owlcotes'.

BARROW-ON-TRENT (South Derbyshire)

SK3528: 6 miles (10km) S of Derby

Barrow-on-Trent, as its name implies, stands between the River Trent and the Trent and Mersey Canal in the rich agricultural land of South Derbyshire. An interesting feature of the village is the row of parish cottages, which were built by parish levy in the 18th century. They were first let at a rent of 30 shillings (£1.50p) a year, and the parish council still keeps them in a good state of repair.

The **church of St Wilfred** is first mentioned in the Domesday Book, but the present building, reached down a pretty lane which goes towards the river, dates mainly from the 13th century. Its most notable feature is the north arcade with its original columns. The church has a light and airy atmosphere, thanks to the plain glass windows. The base of the square tower and the north aisle are 14th century, and there is a Georgian east window. The village chapel, in Chapel Lane, had to be erected on arches to raise it to the level of the road, but was not to the approval of everyone: someone took a shot at it, the marks of which can still be seen in the inscription stone set in the front of the building.

BASLOW (Derbyshire Dales)

SK2572: 4 miles (6km) NE of Bakewell

Standing at the northern gates to Chatsworth, Baslow has been closely linked with the affairs of the Cavendish family for centuries. One of the best hotels in the Peak is Baslow's Devonshire Arms, and at Goose Green and Nether End, you are close to the parklands of Chatsworth, with their lodges by Wyatville.

Baslow clusters beneath its own Peakland 'edge', which provides fine views across the Derwent Valley towards Chatsworth House. The **Wellington Monument** was erected by a local Dr Wrench to celebrate the Duke's victory at Waterloo. The climb to the top of the isolated tor known as the **Eagle Stone** was said to be the test for every young Baslow man before he married.

Today, Baslow is a commuter village for nearby Sheffield and Chesterfield, but it retains its village community spirit despite the roaring traffic of the A623. The **parish church of St Anne** is beautifully situated by the river, and its squat broach spire dominates the village. An unusual feature is the clock face, which has the legend VICTORIA 1897 instead of numbers to mark the Queen's jubilee. Inside the church another unusual feature is preserved, the whip used to drive stray dogs out of the church during services.

Baslow has two fine bridges over the River Derwent. The one at Nether End is a neighbour of one of the few thatched cottages in the Peak District, and the Bridge End bridge, near the church, dates from the 17th century and features a tiny toll-house with an entrance only $3\frac{1}{2}$ft (1m) high.

BEELEY (Derbyshire Dales)

SK2667: 6 miles (10km) N of Matlock

A pretty little 'estate village' for nearby Chatsworth. Most of the stone-built houses date from the 19th century, and many are still owned by the estate and used for housing their workers. The village pub is almost inevitably the Devonshire Arms.

Beeley stands below the moorland wastes of Beeley Moor, where the Bronze Age barrow of **Hob Hurst's House** can now be reached by a concessionary path from Hell Bank, above the village.

The **parish church of St Anne** is a glorious sight in the spring, when the tree-lined churchyard is filled with daffodils. It has a Norman south door, and squat, square tower, but was over-restored by the Victorians between 1882 and 1884. **Beeley Hall** (now a private farm) is an early 17th century, two and a half-storey country house with stone mullioned and transomed windows.

BELPER (Amber Valley)

SK3447: 15 miles (24km) N of Derby

Belper owes its fame and fortune to the Strutt family, for whom the founding father was Jedediah, the wheelwright son of a South Normanton farmer, who set up one of the earliest water-powered cotton mills here in 1776. With the **River Derwent** providing the power, and fuel coming from the nearby South Derbyshire coalfield, the valley has a good claim to be one of the cradles of the Industrial Revolution.

Strutt, who had first made his fortune from the development of ribbed knitting, had gone into profitable partnership with Richard Arkwright, and in 1771, the pair had set up the world's first water-powered cotton mill at Cromford. Strutt and his son, William, retained the North Mill at Belper when

the partnership was dissolved in 1782, having added another at Milford in 1780. The Strutt family were great benefactors to Belper for 150 years, providing work, housing, education and even food from the model farms they set up in the surrounding countryside. Their influence can still be seen in many parts of the town.

The oldest mill still surviving in Belper is the two-storeyed **North Mill** at Bridgefoot, near the main town bridge and magnificent crescent-shaped weir in the Derwent. The old mill, originally built in 1786, has cast-iron columns and beams, and hollow tile floors which provided a warm-air central heating system. It is now a visitor centre, which tells the fascinating story of the Derwent Valley, and is used by a variety of other businesses. The neighbouring, massive, red-brick **East Mill** was constructed in 1912, but now is largely empty. A terracotta Jubilee Tower was erected on the mill site in 1897 to mark Queen Victoria's jubilee.

All that train travellers on the Midland line see of Belper is George Stephenson's mile-long cutting, walled throughout in gritstone and spanned by no less than ten bridges. It was an engineering wonder of the day when completed in 1840.

Despite this industrial past, the name of Belper is derived from the French *beau repaire*, meaning 'beautiful retreat', and there are still some lovely waterside walks in this bustling little town.

Among the other interesting buildings in the town are the **Christ Church**, a lofty, spacious Victorian church built in 1849; the **parish**

church of St Peter, built with a pinnacled west tower and in a Commissioner's style by Habershon in 1824 and the **chapel of St John the Baptist** in The Butts, which is the earliest of all, dating from 1683. **George Brettle's Warehouse**, in Chapel Street, was built in a dignified, classical style in 1834, and his monument can be seen in St Peter's Church.

BIRCHOVER
(Derbyshire Dales)

SK2462: 5 miles (8km) S of Bakewell

The main street of Birchover climbs gently up from the weird outcrops of Rowtor Rocks at the foot of the village and heads towards the heights of neighbouring Stanton Moor. The name accurately describes this hillside village, and means the 'birch-covered steep slope'.

Birchover was the home of **J.C. and J.P. Heathcote**, father and son amateur antiquarians who systematically investigated the monuments and barrows on Stanton Moor (cf. Stanton-in-the-Peak) and kept a fascinating private museum in the old village post office in the main street. The Heathcote collection is now in Sheffield's Weston Park Museum.

Prehistory is rife in the vicinity of Birchover, and the weird rocks of Rowtor, behind The Druid Inn, are said to have been used for Druidical rites. Whether they were or not is open to question, but the **Reverend Thomas Eyre**, who died in 1717, was certainly fascinated by them. It was he who built the strange collection of steps, rooms and seats which have been carved out of the gritstone rocks on the summit of the

outcrop. It is said that he took his friends there to admire the view across the valley below – a view now sadly obscured by trees. More recently, prehistoric **cup-and-ring marks** have been discovered on the rocks, which also boasted a rocking stone.

Thomas Eyre lived at the Old Vicarage in the village below Rowtor Rocks and built the charming little church known as the Jesus Chapel or Rowtor Chapel, beneath the rocks. The chapel had been demoted to the village cheese store before Eyre's restoration, and it now features, among fragments of Norman work, strange carvings and decorations. These include modern stained glass by Brian Clarke, the internationally famous artist who lived at the vicarage for a time in the 1970s.

Nearby are the equally strange outcrops of **Robin Hood's Stride** or Mock Beggar's Hall, and **Cratcliff Tor**, at the foot of which a medieval hermit's cave, complete with crucifix, can still be found hidden behind a venerable yew.

BOLSOVER (Bolsover)

SK4770: 6 miles (10km) east of Chesterfield

Pevsner remarked that not many large houses in England occupy such an impressive position as **Bolsover Castle** (English Heritage), standing as it does on the brow of a hill overlooking the valley of the River Rother and Doe Lea. There have been many changes in the landscape since Pevsner described it, the most important of which are the disappearance of most of the coal mines and the construction of the M1, which now slices noisily across the view.

The first castle at Bolsover was built by William Peverel, the illegitimate son of William the Conqueror, as part of his vast Derbyshire estates. Nothing remains of that Norman building, and what the visitor sees today is mainly the result of Sir Charles Cavendish's romantic rebuilding of 1613-16. Inside the 17th-century 'keep' or 'Little Castle' are a series of remarkable rooms, including the Vaulted Hall, the Pillar Room, the Star Chamber, the Elysium and the Heaven Room, many of which have ornate chimney pieces, panelling or paintings. Sir Charles's son, William, was responsible for the eastern range of buildings known as the Riding School, and the roofless but still impressive western terrace. The whole building later descended to the Dukes of Portland, and it is now in the care of English Heritage. Bolsover Castle is a strangely impressive place, even now threatened by its industrial surroundings and constantly troubled by subsidence, the legacy of centuries of coal mining beneath its walls.

Across the road from the castle is the **Hudson Bay** public house. Its name recalls the fact that it was originally built by Peter Fidler, a Bolsover man who was a distinguished surveyor with the Hudson Bay Company in Canada during the 18th century. A Peter Fidler Society still exists in Canada today. The **White Swan** is probably Bolsover's oldest public house, and is said to have served as the moot hall from the Middle Ages to the early 19th century. Bolsover was granted its market charter by Henry III in 1225.

The **parish church of St Mary** dates from the 13th century, and the main sources of interest, following a Victorian restoration after a fire in 1897, are the Cavendish monuments in the eponymous Cavendish Chapel. These include two magnificent tombs to Charles Cavendish, who died in 1617, and Henry Cavendish, who died in 1727. Buried in the churchyard are John Smythson and Huntingdon Smythson, the 17th-century architects who were probably responsible for the design of the rebuilt Bolsover Castle.

BONSALL (Derbyshire Dales)

SK2758: 2 miles (3km) SE of Matlock

Bonsall is a charming former lead mining village clustered around its ball-topped 17th-century cross. This is encircled by thirteen gritstone steps, in the steeply sloping market square. Set in a steep-sided dale beneath Masson Hill, Bonsall was famous as a lead mining centre, and many of the fields and meadows around are still littered with the remains of the miners' work.

Beside the cross stands the **King's Head Inn**, which dates from 1677 and is said to be haunted. The other pubs in the village reflect the traditional occupations of its residents, they are the Pig of Lead and the Barley Mow. Above the village centre stands the battlemented parish church of St James, with its distinguished Perpendicular pinnacled tower and spire. Most of the church was built in the 13th century, and a beautiful clerestory lights the nave. The Baptist Chapel dates from 1824.

The beautifully wooded road up from Cromford is known as the Via Gellia, but contrary to the belief of many, it is not Roman. It was named after the Gell family of Hopton by Philip Gell, who built the road in the 1790s to carry lead and stone from his mines and quarries to the Cromford Canal. The name was later adapted to 'Viyella' by the owners of the former Hollin Mill when they invented a new brand of hosiery.

BORROWASH (Erewash)

SK 4134: 5 miles (8km) E of Derby

Now swallowed up by the suburban sprawl between Derby and Nottingham, Borrowash (pronounced 'borrow--ash') retains a village air despite the constant roar of traffic on the A52. In the recent past, Borrowash has lost its railway station and canal. The latter was filled in the early 1960s.

The small, red-brick **church of St Stephen** was designed by P.H. Currey in 1899, and features inside a low, 18th-century ironwork chancel screen, which is thought to be the work of Robert Bakewell of Derby.

BOYLESTONE (Derbyshire Dales)

SK1835: 8 miles (13km) S of Ashbourne

Boylestone is an isolated village in the gently rolling countryside to the south of Ashbourne. History may have passed it by but for an incident during the Civil War, when 200 Royalist troops spent the night in the **church of St John the Baptist** on their way to the relief of Wingfield Manor. Foolishly, they set no watch, and in the morning found themselves surrounded by Cromwell's men. They surrendered and were disarmed as they sheepishly filed out of the church.

The Victorian church tower has an unusual pyramidal roof, but inside, the chancel is as the Cavaliers would have seen it, for it dates to the 14th century, as does a finely moulded, low recess in the chancel. There is a tablet to Herbert Croft who died in 1785 on the north wall of the nave.

BRACKENFIELD (North East Derbyshire)

SK3759: 4 miles (6km) E of Matlock

Known as Brackenthwaite in the Middle Ages, the name means 'clearing in the bracken'. The village is perhaps best known today for the **Ogston Reservoir,** which was built in 1960. The site of the former Ogston Mill was submerged under the rising waters, and hidden in the surrounding trees is the ruin of the former Trinity Chapel. This was mentioned in the Domesday Book, but was abandoned when the new church was built in 1856. The ancient screen was removed from the chapel to the new church. The reservoir is overlooked by romantic **Ogston Hall**, which dates from the 16th century and was the ancestral home of the Revell and Turbutt families. The house, extensively altered in 1768, was modernised and medievalised in Victorian times.

BRADBOURNE (Derbyshire Dales)

SK2052: 5 miles (8km) NE of Ashbourne

People have worshipped in this tiny village for over 1000 years, as is evidenced by the venerable stump of the Saxon carved cross in the churchyard. This cross shows an image of the Crucifixion and there is more Saxon work in the **church of All Saints**, especially on the north side of the nave where typical long-and-short work is visible. The massive, four-square unbuttressed west tower is of Norman date and has a finely decorated south door. Most of the rest of this charming little church dates from the 14th century, but there are fine modern furnishings which owe much to William Morris's Arts and Crafts movement. Some of the wall paintings date from the 17th and 18th centuries.

East of the church stands the Elizabethan, grey stone **Bradbourne Hall** (private) with its three gables and beautiful terraced gardens.

BRADLEY (Derbyshire Dales)

SK2145: 3 miles (5km) E of Ashbourne

Dr Samuel Johnson was a regular visitor to the Meynell family at the Georgian **Bradley Hall** (private) when he was staying in Ashbourne with his friend, Dr John Taylor. The Meynells came to Bradley in 1655, when they bought the hall from Sir Andrew Kniveton, who had been financially ruined by the Civil War.

The hall stands opposite the **church of All Saints**, which is notable for having a bell turret, but no tower on its 14th-century nave and chancel. The original wooden bell tower was destroyed when it was struck by lightning. There are many memorials to the Meynell family in the church, including a rare hatchment. The base and part of the

shaft of a Saxon cross stand in the churchyard.

The archway which crosses the formerly gated road between cottages at Moorend is known locally as 'The Hole in the Wall'. The village pub has the unusual distinction of having two official names, The Jinglers and the Fox and Hounds. Nearby Bradley Wood was given to the people of Ashbourne for their recreation by Captain Fitzherbert Wright in 1935.

BRADWELL (Derbyshire Dales)

SK1781: 3 miles (2km) SE of Castleton

Bradwell – usually abbreviated in the way of Peak District villages to 'Bradder' – is a charming, little limestone village sheltering under the glider-haunted escarpment of Bradwell Edge. It owes its fortune to the lead mining industry of the 18th and 19th centuries, when it was near the centre of a rich lead mining area. Most Peak District lead miners also wore a Bradwell product – the hard, black, brimmed hat in which they stuck their candles to light their way underground were universally known as 'Bradder beavers'. And Bradwell's final claim to fame is that it was the birthplace in 1815 of Samuel Fox, the inventor of the folding-frame umbrella. Bradwell has also made cotton goods, telescopes and spectacles during its industrial history.

Bradwell's long and fascinating history goes back at least as far as the Romans. They built the small fort known as **Navio** on the banks of the River Noe, north of the village in what is now the hamlet of Brough, during the first century AD, probably to defend their lead mining interests in the area. There is a persistent local legend originating from Castleton that the people of Bradwell were Roman slaves, and this may be a long-held folk memory of the civilian vicus which once existed outside the walls of Navio.

During the troubled period after the Romans left, the mysterious **Grey Ditch**, a broad fortification north of the village, was built, perhaps to defend Bradford Dale and the village against the Hope Valley. But no one really knows why it was built or by whom. Another local legend is that Bradwell was the scene of a Dark Age battle, after which the Saxon King Edwin was murdered by being hung from a tree. The local name of 'Eden Tree' is said to get its name from the spot.

A reminder of Bradwell's lead mining days is the **Bagshawe Cavern,** which was discovered above the village by lead miners in 1806 and is now open to the public, with special 'adventure' caving trips for the brave.

A mile south of the village, at the head of the rock-rimmed Bradwell Dale, is **Hazelbadge Hall.** This attractive, old, stone-built manor house dates from 1549 and was part of the dowry which Dorothy Vernon of Haddon Hall gave to her new husband, John Manners.

BRAILSFORD
(Derbyshire Dales)

SK2541: 7 miles (11km) NW of Derby

Bisected by the A52, midway between Derby and Ashbourne, Brailsford is a pretty, red-brick village which was im-portant enough to be mentioned in the Domesday Book as having a priest and 'half a church'. The owner then was Elfin, who appears to have been a Saxon who managed to retain his lord-ship after the Conquest. Dating from Elfin's time is the carved Saxon cross shaft in the churchyard of **All Saints Parish Church,** an interesting build-ing with much Norman work and an ashlar-faced, diagonally buttressed tower.

Nearby at Mugginton is the so-called **Halter Devil Chapel,** now part of a farm and built, if the legend is to be be-lieved, by a reformed drunkard who once tried to halter a cow which he mis-takenly thought was his horse. In his drunken stupor, the farmer, Francis Browen, thought he had haltered the Devil and is said to have built the chapel in 1723 in repentance. The ham-let of **Ednaston,** on the other side of the Brailsford Brook, has a manor built by Sir Edward Lutyens, but it is not open to the public.

BRASSINGTON
(Derbyshire Dales)

SK2354: 4 miles (6km) west of Wirksworth

In the heart of lead mining country, the landscape around Brassington's hill-top, stone-built cottages is littered with the remains of 't'owd man'. The bumps and hollows in the green mead-ows tell of 200 years of underground industry in pursuit of the precious ga-lena – or lead ore – and they now flower with lead-tolerant flowers such as mountain pansy, sandwort and orchids.

The oldest 'resident' of Brassington

is the relief carving of a man with one hand over his heart inside the Norman tower of the **parish church of St James**. It may be Saxon in date, but most of the rest of the church is Norman, with a very fine south arcade and Perpendicular windows, but heavily restored by the Victorians. Nearby is the **Wesleyan Reform Chapel**, one of the so-called 'Smedley Chapels' built in 1852 by the local millowner, Mr Smedley, a keen Revivalist. Of the two other chapels in the village, one now serves as the village hall and the other is a private house.

Nearby is much attractive limestone countryside on the southern edge of the Peak District National Park. Attractions include **Rainster** and **Harborough Rocks**, Dolomitic limestone crags in whose caves and crevices have been found evidence of prehistoric man.

BREADSALL (Erewash)

SK3639: 2 miles (3km) N of Derby

Once a small hamlet clustered around its Norman church, Breadsall is now very much a residential suburb of Derby, with new estates which have sprung up around the original centre. The **parish church of All Saints** has one of the finest and most elegant steeples in the county, dating from the early years of the 14th century. The south doorway is Norman and the tower and chancel are 13th century. The church has an interesting recent history, apparently being burnt down by suffragettes in 1914, and carefully restored over the next two years. Why the suffragettes should choose this quiet backwater for their protest is not explained. Inside

there is a touching pieta dating from the late 14th century, which shows the Virgin Mary with the crucified Christ lying across her knees. The beautiful alabaster sculpture was miraculously found under the floor of the church after another fire, and was restored to its present position by W.D. Caroe.

The **Old Hall**, opposite the west end of the church, has a chequered history, but has been part of village life for 600 years. Parts of it date to the 14th century, and it was originally the manor house, when the village was divided into the wards of Overhall and Netherhall. In later years, it has been a farmhouse, hunting box, school, shop, public house, joiner's shop and post office. It currently serves as a parish hall and is used by various village organisations.

Breadsall Priory (now a private hotel with a golf course) stands on the site of an Augustinian Priory which was founded in the 13th century. Only an arch of this original building survives in the basement of the present one, which is mainly Jacobean with many early 19th-century additions and embellishments. Breadsall Priory was the home in his later years of **Erasmus Darwin** (b1731), the physician, poet and philosopher, and grandfather of Charles Darwin. He died here in 1802. There is a memorial to him in All Saints Church.

BREASTON (Erewash)

SK4533: 7 miles (11km) E of Derby

On the southern borders of the county, close to Nottinghamshire and Leicestershire, Breaston lies in the flat countryside close to where the Derwent joins the Trent on its long journey to the North Sea. It is now almost a suburb of Long Eaton, which itself is a southern suburb of the great city of Nottingham.

An interesting feature in the mainly 13th-century **church of St Michael** is the so-called 'Boy of Breaston' – a small, chubby-faced lad immortalised by the mason of the nave arches in the 13th century, and who has smiled down on worshippers and visitors ever since. The story is that while the church was being built, this boy would come and sit, chin in his hands, and watch the masons at work. The master mason decided that he would ensure that this cheeky spectator would always have a good view of the church – so he made him part of it!

There was no burial ground at Breaston until 1824, and coffins had to be carried to neighbouring Church Wilne for burial. The footpath over the fields of Wilne is still known by villagers as the 'Coffin Walk'. Memories of the now drained Derby Canal, which passed through the village, are still revived by the Navigation Inn. Here, the basin where the narrowboats were turned can still be seen.

BRETBY (South Derbyshire)

SK2923: 3 miles (2km) E of Burton-on-Trent

The Norse name of the village means 'the farm of the Britons', and probably refers to the Britons who accompanied the Scandinavians when they first settled in this spot above the valley of the Trent, near the present border with Staffordshire.

The Mount is the centre of Bretby, and it was here, during the 13th century, that a castle and the original church were built. Nothing now remains of either, although parts of the old church still remain in the 19th-century **St Wystan's Church**. The view from The Mount is justly famous and extends for up to 40 miles across the Trent Valley. The hill was used as a beacon for many centuries. The later history of Bretby is tied up with coal mining and the Bretby Colliery produced coal for about 100 years but that too has gone.

Bretby Park, with its 600-acre park, was originally built for the 2nd Earl of Chesterfield to a design by Inigo Jones, but this fine house was demolished in the 18th century. The replacement mock-Gothic house was erected between 1812 and 1813 by Sir Jeffrey Wyatville, and is now used as a hospital. One of the longest lasting legends of Bretby is that of the cedar of Lebanon which formerly stood in the grounds. It was thought to be one of the oldest cedars in the country, being planted in 1676, and for many years it was held up by the chains which eventually killed it. When a branch fell from the cedar, it was said that it presaged the death of a member of the family.

BUXTON (High Peak)

SK0673: 5 miles (8km) S of Chapel-en-le-Frith

If it had been a few feet lower and had a slightly kinder climate, Buxton might have rivalled Bath or Cheltenham as a fashionable spa town. As it is, its altitude of around 1000ft (300m) above the sea and its frequent appearances in severe winter weather forecasts have cast Buxton in the role of a slightly faded spa, which never quite won the popularity of its southern counterparts.

The Romans were the first to realise the health-giving qualities of Buxton's warm (28°C) springs. They were also the first to take advantage of these natural aquifers, naming the town Aquae Arnemetiae – 'the spa of the goddess of the grove'. Later, the waters were taken by pilgrims from all over Britain, most notably Mary Queen of Scots, forcibly detained at Chatsworth for so many years, but a frequent visitor to the Old Hall, now a hotel. She also is said to have visited the natural caverns known as Poole's Cavern on Green Lane, where her 'chair' is still pointed out. It is here that the first evidence of Man's presence in the Buxton area has been found, in the prehistoric remains

The Opera House

founds near the cave entrance. Above the cavern is the **Grin Low Country Park** and the prominent folly and viewpoint known as Solomon's Temple.

Buxton really came into national prominence when the major landowner, the 5th Duke of Devonshire from Chatsworth, invested large sums of money in the development of Buxton as a spa. Much of the money came from the proceeds of his very profitable copper mines in the Manifold Valley. The magnificent, sweeping, golden sandstone Crescent, designed by John Carr of York on the model of John Wood's Royal Crescent in Bath, was built in 1784. It was originally three hotels for the use of spa visitors. It was recently restored by English Heritage and others, but is still a fine building looking for a viable modern use.

The **Natural Baths** (now shops) and **St Ann's Well** were also renovated in the late 18th century, and in 1790, the 5th Duke built the Great Stables and Riding School on the slope behind the Crescent. In 1858, the 6th Duke converted this magnificent building, in its time the largest unsupported dome in the world, into a hospital, which it still is today, known as the **Devonshire Royal Hospital.**

The elegant Italian-style **parish church of St John the Baptist** was built in 1811 by Sir Jeffrey Wyatville. It has a fine Tuscan-columned portico on its west front and a beautiful tower with a domed top. In the same year, Wyatville laid out the area below the Market Place in Upper Buxton as The Slopes, where patients taking the waters could enjoy some gentle exercise. Behind The Slopes, the grand **Town**

Hall (1887-9) dominates the Market Place, with the interesting and award-winning **Buxton Museum** further down on Terrace Road, which leads to The Crescent.

The heyday of Buxton's popularity as a spa came with the opening of the Midland Line in 1863. The imposing **Palace Hotel** was built by the 7th Duke in 1868 to cater for the growth in tourism. This was closely followed by the **Pavilion** and **Pavilion Gardens** in 1871, and the gloriously ornate **Opera House**, built to a design by Frank Matcham, in 1905. The Opera House is now the home of the annual international **Buxton Festival of Music and the Arts**, and opera is still the mainstay of this wonderful little 'theatre in the hills'.

CALDWELL
(South Derbyshire)

SK2517: 3 miles (5km) W of Swadlincote

Caldwell is a quiet village tucked away among the lanes of South Derbyshire. The small but charming **parish church of St Giles** has three narrow, round-headed windows on the north side of the nave which could be Saxon. Most of the rest of the church dates from Norman times, and the west window has two roundels of stained glass which were made in Nuremberg in Germany and date from around 1400. They show the Resurrection and Joab slaying Abner.

Caldwell Hall, an eleven-bay, parapeted, brick mansion which is now a special school, was built in the 17th century on grounds which were surrounded by a moat. It was owned by the Evans family of Burton-on-Trent, and later became a country club.

CALKE (South Derbyshire)

SK3722: 6 miles (10km) NE of Swadlincote

For many years, the early 18th century Baroque country mansion of **Calke Abbey** (National Trust) was one of the great unknown secrets of the Derbyshire countryside. Lying in an isolated hollow and surrounded by extensive grounds grazed by a flock of rare Portland sheep, Calke Abbey stands on the site of an Augustinian priory, but was a private house for most of its long life. Most of the houses in the small hamlet, which is dominated by the **Staunton Harold Reservoir** to the north, are associated with the estate. There are fine views across the reservoir from the car park at the end of the cul-de-sac road through the village.

The Harpur Crewe family had lived here since 1622, and the present house was built by Sir John Harpur in 1703 to replace his former house at Swarkestone. Generations of Harpurs lived out their lives as virtual recluses in this glorious isolation, latterly Sir Vauncey Harpur Crewe, who died in 1924. They were great collectors, and when the National Trust took over the house from Mr Henry Harpur Crewe in 1985, they discovered an untouched time capsule of furniture, natural history specimens and other objets d'art left just as they had been since the 1920s. After several years of careful, but sympathetic, restoration by the Trust, the house was opened to the public. It now provides a fascinating insight into the lives of the members of one of the county's more eccentric landowning families and their accumulative passions.

The abbey itself consists of a three-storey, eleven-bay south front with a grand pedimented, four-column Ionic portico. The three-bay angled pavilions project and are flanked by fluted Ionic pilasters, which are repeated on the western and eastern sides of the house. The house is thought to be to a design by Francis Smith of Warwick, or his brother, William. Entrance to the house is by timed ticket because of the nature of the exhibits inside.

The **church of St Giles,** in the grounds of the house, was built in 1826, and has a narrow west tower and castellated nave. Inside is a monument to Sir John Harpur, the original builder of the house, which is dated 1741.

CALVER (Derbyshire Dales)

SK2374: 5 miles (8km) N of Bakewell

Sheltering in the Derwent Valley below Curbar Edge, Calver (pronounced 'carver') is a pleasant little stone-built village with some attractive old gritstone cottages and a fine 18th-century bridge over the river. Its most impressive building is undoubtedly **Calver Mill**, a magnificent, six-storeyed cotton mill first built in 1785. The present building mainly dates from a rebuilding following a fire of 1805. Internally it has cast-iron pillars holding up the floors, which were originally of wood. There is a preserved Wheel House from the original mill. Cotton was produced here until 1923, when it was bought by a Sheffield company which specialises in stainless steel products. Calver Mill,

which is private, reached a far wider audience when it represented Colditz Castle in the popular television series about the famous prisoner of war camp of the same name.

Calver Sough and the former Calver Sough Mine are at the northern end of the village, and recall the days when lead mining was such an important plank of the local economy. (In Derbyshire, a 'sough' – pronounced 'suff'- is an underground drain constructed to take water away from lead mines.) Nearby is the Derbyshire Craft Centre, which has a shop, gallery and restaurant for tourists.

CARSINGTON (Derbyshire Dales)

SK2552: 2 miles (3km) W of Wirksworth

Carsington is now inextricably associated with its huge reservoir. This was built by Severn-Trent Water and opened by the Queen in 1992. The **reservoir** is the centre for a wide range of water-based activities and recreations, including sailing, birdwatching and windsurfing. The popular walk around the shores is 9 miles (14km) long, and there is also an award-winning visitor centre with plenty of interactive exhibits which tell the story of water engineering and are guaranteed to keep the youngsters occupied.

During the troubled and long-drawn-out building of the reservoir, archaeologists discovered a Romano-British in the area, which some claim might have been the long-lost Ludutarum – the centre for Roman lead mining in the Peak District.

Although dominated by the reservoir, Carsington village still has some pleasant cottages and an interesting **parish church of St Margaret**, situated at the foot of the open 1000-ft hill known as Carsington Pastures. Originally built during the 12th century, St Margaret's was rebuilt, or 're-edified' as the sundial in the south wall puts it, in 1648. It has three straight-headed Perpendicular windows and memorials to the Gells of nearby Hopton. An interesting entry in the church register mentions Sarah Tissington, who died in 1668 after having been born without hands or arms, yet who learned to knit, dig the garden and do other things with her feet.

CASTLETON (High Peak)

SK1582: 6 miles (10km) E of Chapel-en-le-Frith

Castleton's fame lies in its splendid situation, surrounded by the hills and standing at the geological junction of the White and Dark Peak at the head of the beautiful Hope Valley. The little township dates from the 12th century, when it was laid out beneath Peveril Castle to a gridiron plan. It was situated inside a Town Ditch, parts of which can still be seen to the north, west and east of the village centre. But the village grew up depending on and in the shadow of William Peverel's commanding castle and never quite filled the boundaries laid down by its planners.

Castleton owes its fortune to Peverel's masterful choice for the siting of his castle. It was probably primarily built to control the countryside and, in particular, his lead mining interests in

Castleton Parish Church

the area, but also to administer his hunting preserve of the Royal Forest of the Peak.

Peveril Castle (English Heritage) was begun in the years immediately following the Conquest and is one of the first stone-built castles in the country. The herringbone masonry of the northern curtain wall, facing the village, shows some of this earliest Norman work. The splendid but roofless keep was built by Henry II in the 1170s. He had received the submission of King Malcolm of Scotland at Peveril on one of his many hunting visits in 1157, and for him it always remained a favourite castle. The entrance to the castle in Henry's day was from the west, across a bridge which spanned the top of the Peak Cavern gorge. Today's visitors have to toil up the modern zigzag path from the village centre to the north. There are fine views from Peveril's ramparts, especially looking north to the Great Ridge of Back Tor and Lose Hill, and west towards what was perhaps the first administrative centre of Castleton, the great hill fort which encircles the lofty summit of **Mam Tor**. This is at the head of the valley and dates from the late Bronze and early Iron Age.

The village of Castleton depends largely on the tourist trade for its livelihood today, and the four show caves of Peak Cavern, Treak Cliff, Speedwell and Blue John receive thousands of visitors every year. The oldest of Castleton's show caves is **Peak Cavern**, directly beneath the castle, which is said to have the largest cave entrance in Britain. A whole community of ropemakers lived in this 'village which never saw the sun' in the vast cave entrance, and there are plans to restore rope-making demonstrations here. **Treak Cliff**, on the road to Mam Tor which is now closed, has some marvellous formations. **Blue John**, beneath the east face of Mam Tor, is named after the semi-precious banded fluorspar which is found here and sold as ornaments and jewellery in the town's many trinket shops. **Speedwell Cavern**, which uniquely is reached by a boat, is at the foot of the **Winnats Pass** (National Trust). This spectacular dry limestone gorge takes the main road from the west into Castleton since the collapse of the Mam Tor road.

Many people believe that the **parish church of St Edmund** in Castle Street was originally built by the same architect who built the castle. There is certainly a resemblance in the ornamentation of the chancel arch and

that on the eastern gateway to the castle. St Edmund's may have been the garrison church to the castle, but it is an interesting church in its own right, complete with 17th-century box pews – a rarity in Derbyshire. Unfortunately, it suffered from a heavy-handed restoration in 1837. Across the road is the 17th-century Castle Hotel, said to be haunted by a young woman, and just up the street in the Market Square is **Castleton Hall**, a fine 17th-century house now converted to a youth hostel.

CHADDESDEN (Derby)

SK3737: 2 miles (3km) E of Derby

Chaddesden, once the Derbyshire seat of the powerful Wilmot family, is now not much more than a commuter village for neighbouring Derby and Nottingham. Nothing remains of Tudor Chaddesden Hall, a yellow-brick building which was founded by Robert Wilmot in the 16th century, but which was demolished as recently as the 1920s. The public park known as Mosey Yard occupies the site today, and there is a children's paddling pool where the Wilmots raised their fish for the table in their fishponds. The name of the Wilmot family is perpetuated in the Wilmot Arms public house on Morley Road. Chaddesden was the site of much overspill housing for Derby in the 1950s and 1960s.

Chaddesden's **parish church of St Mary** is interesting because it is a dated example of Decorated church architecture, built before the Perpendicular style became popular. The church was rebuilt by Henry Chaddesden, Archdeacon of Leicester, around 1357, and the tall and spacious chancel, running from its nave and aisles, dates from this period. The great west tower, with its angle buttresses and large west door, is definitely Perpendicular in style.

CHAPEL-EN-LE-FRITH (High Peak)

SK0580: 5 miles (8km) N of Buxton

Chapel-en-le-Frith proudly announces itself as 'The Capital of the Peak', but the name comes from the Norman French and actually means 'the chapel in the forest'. This is a reference to the **Royal Forest of the Peak**, which extended over much of North Derbyshire during the Middle Ages and was used by medieval kings and princes for their sport. Chapel has been described as one of the best-kept secrets of the Peak District, and it certainly hides its charms away from the fleeting passer-by. The opening of the Chapel-en-le-Frith by-

pass in 1987 means that even more people miss this charming and ancient market town as they rush between Buxton and Stockport.

The first chapel was built here for the foresters in 1225, and later it was dedicated to **St Thomas à Becket**, as the present, mainly 14th-century, parish church still is. But the first medieval church was extensively modernised in 1733 by George Platt of Rotherham, who created the crumbling but still dignified Georgian exterior, with its classical porch topped by a sundial, that we see today. The interior of the building features 19th-century box pews and the monument to **William Bagshawe** of nearby Ford Hall, who was known as 'the Apostle of the Peak' for his evangelistic work as a Nonconformist minister during the latter part of the 17th century.

One of the most gruesome episodes in the church's long history occurred in 1648, when 1500 Scottish soldiers

Chapel-en-le-Frith market place

taken prisoner after the Battle of Ribbleton Moor were locked in the church for two weeks. Forty-eight died in what became known as 'The Black Hole of Derbyshire'. In the churchyard is a simple slab marked by the letters 'PL' and the outline of an axe. It is tempting to think that this so-called 'Woodcutter's Grave' marks the burial place of one of the original foresters of the Royal Forest of the Peak.

The main road through the town, Market Street, always passed below the sloping, cobbled Market Square, which is the real centre of Chapel and a delightful place. It is surrounded by a range of interesting old inns and buildings, and watched over by an ancient cross which may have stood there for over 500 years and the recently renovated village stocks. Church Brow, which leads down from the church to Market Street, is a charming thoroughfare, steep and cobbled, and looking as though it has been transported from a postcard from the West Country.

Chapel's modern fortune is based on the huge Ferodo brake linings factory west of the town. This was founded a century ago by local man Herbert Froode (of which 'Ferodo' is an anagram) who first developed a brake block for the horse-drawn carts which then plied across the steep Derbyshire hills. Chapel was formerly a centre of the boot and shoe making industry, which strangely enough gave rise to the modern term 'brake shoes'.

A couple of miles to the north-east of the town, on a former Pennine farm, is the **Chestnut Centre**, a wildlife conservation centre famous for its otters, where visitors can view native wildlife at close quarters in pleasant surroundings.

CHARLESWORTH (High Peak)

SK0092: 2 miles (3km) SW of Glossop

Charlesworth stands on the western edge of the Pennines, south-west of Glossop, and has the unusual distinction in this land of Nonconformism of having a Congregational Chapel which was virtually the parish church for 200 years. This was before the building in 1849 of the present mock-Gothic **parish church of St John the Baptist**. The present rather grand Congregational Chapel, with its large graveyard, dominates the village, and was built in 1797 on the site of the original 13th-century chapel of Charlesworth. It is known in the village as the 'Top Chapel' because of its position on the hill at the top of Long Lane. The Catholic church, built in 1895 chiefly to serve the many Irish immigrants who worked in the nearby mills, stands in a beautiful position on the banks of the River Etherow on the edge of the village.

Many of the older cottages in Charlesworth are typically Pennine buildings of three storeys and were originally built as cottages for weavers, who processed the cloth brought from the mills in nearby Stockport and Manchester. **Best Hill Bridge**, at the foot of the village, certainly seems to have been built for packhorses rather than modern traffic.

CHELMORTON (Derbyshire Dales)

SK1169: 4 miles (6km) SE of Buxton

Twin Bronze Age burial mounds on the airy, 1463ft (446m) summit of **Chel-**

morton Low watch over the hillside village of Chelmorton – or 'Chelly' as it affectionately known locally. Chelmorton Low dominates what is one of the highest villages not only in Derbyshire, but the whole country. The stream which runs down from the Low and through the centre of this one-street village has the charming name of Illy Willy Water. The medieval strip field systems of Chelmorton, 'fossilised' by drystone walls which were built at the time of the enclosures and which still run back from the village crofts, are a nationally famous historic landscape, now in the process of being protected by the Peak District National Park Authority.

The **parish church of St John the Baptist**, built into the side of the hill, is one of the most interesting in the county. The elegant 15th-century spire is recessed on its 13th-century tower and is topped by a weathervane in the form of a locust – a reminder of the Baptist's time in the wilderness. Parts of this fine old church, including the south arcade, date from the early 13th century, and it boasts the real rarity of a complete 14th-century, Perpendicular-style, stone chancel screen. In the stone-vaulted south porch is a gallery of early sculptures and grave slabs, some of which may be Saxon, as is the broken shaft of an old cross in the sloping churchyard.

CHESTERFIELD (Chesterfield)

SK3871: 12 miles (20km) S of Sheffield

Forever associated with the famous twisted spire of its cathedral-sized, mainly 14th-century parish church,

Chesterfield has a history which extends back to Roman times. Derbyshire's second-biggest town began as a Roman fort, protecting the lead mining interests of the Empire on the edge of the Peak District. The history of the town is effectively told in the town's excellent **Museum and Art Gallery** in St Mary's Gate in the town centre.

Chesterfield's modern fortune was founded on its industry and the proximity of the Derbyshire coalfield, which fuelled the iron foundries, engineering and other factories which formed the manufacturing base of the town during the 19th and 20th centuries. Chesterfield has always been a hard-working, industrial town, but it recently attracted national recognition and a European Casa Nostra award for the redevelopment of its splendid Market Place. The Market Place was fortunately saved from unsuitable modern development by an upsurge of local public opinion. Today it is a busy, bustling place, with colourful stalls watched over by the tall, red-brick clock tower of the Market Hall, built in 1857. The former Peacock Inn in Low Pavement, a medieval, half-timbered building, was scheduled for demolition, but was saved and now enjoys a new life as the Peacock Information Centre. Other important modern buildings in the town centre include the stylish new County Library; the striking, circular, multi-gabled Court House; and the Peacock Centre in New Beetwell Street. The commanding and handsome Town Hall, dignified by its gracious portico, was built in red brick and stone in 1938. Many of the town centre streets have names which reflect their history, such as The Shambles, but the half-timbered shops in Knifesmithgate and Glumangate date from between the wars. There are some good 18th-century terraces in Saltergate, a name which is a reminder of the valuable product which was brought across the Pennines from Cheshire by packhorse trains. Saltergate is also the home of Chesterfield's famous giant-killing football team, which reached the semi-final of the FA Cup in 1997.

The **parish church of St Mary and All Saints** testifies to the prosperity of the town's many tradesmen's guilds during the 13th and 14th centuries. The interior includes many fine monuments, especially those to the Tudor Foljambe family at the east end of the Lady Chapel. No one is quite sure when the 228ft (69m) spire took on its eccentric, and from certain viewpoints, alarming, twist. The tower and spire were built at the end of the 13th century, and it is thought that the twisting occurred as a result of the effects of the sun warping the lead-covered, unseasoned timbers. The local legend is that it was caused by the Devil getting his tail caught on the spire while flying over the town.

Of the many other Chesterfield churches, the most important is **Holy Trinity** in Newbold Road, a Victorian Gothic structure which was the last resting place of one of Chesterfield's most famous sons, the steam power pioneer George Stephenson, of *Rocket* fame. Stephenson lived for the last years of his life at the red-brick, Georgian **Tapton House**, north-west of the town centre. The Roman Catholic **Church of The Annunciation** in Spencer Street, has a Continental-style west end which was added in 1874 to Joseph Hansom's 1854 building. The Methodist church of 1870, in Saltergate, has a spectacular Renaissance front with an Ionic-columned portico and pediment. The lovely wooded surroundings of Queen's Park are used by Derbyshire County Cricket Club for one of its grounds. This is reached from the town centre by a footbridge formed by a graceful arch of pre-stressed concrete.

CHINLEY (High Peak)

SK0382: 2 miles (3km) W of Chapel-en-le-Frith

Once described as one of the greatest monuments to Victorian industrial England, the twin, curved **Chinley Viaducts**, which sweep over the A6 and A624, are by far the most impressive structures in this small North Derbyshire village. The lines from Derby to Manchester and Sheffield joined here, making Chinley Station, built in 1902, an important junction for passengers to Manchester, Liverpool, London and Sheffield. At one time, up to 180 trains a day passed through the station, which had five waiting rooms (each with a roaring fire), a refreshment room and a bookstall.

Chinley Chapel, built in 1667, is a rare survival of a 17th-century independent place of worship. From the outside, this two-storey building looks like any other house, but behind its mullioned windows is a large, galleried chapel. The Methodist church – known here as 'The Preaching Room' – dates from 1862, and replaced a shop at Chinley End where John Wesley was once entertained.

The associated village of **Buxworth** was formerly known as Bugsworth or

Buggesworth, but apparently the parish council grew tired of being the butt of jokes about bugs, and had the name changed to Buxworth – presumably to be associated with Buxton – in 1929. During the 19th century, Buxworth (then Bugsworth) was a busy little inland port, the terminus for the Peak Forest Tramway and the Peak Forest Canal, which were built in 1806 and linked to the River Mersey. Up to 70 narrow boats a week, carrying coal, limestone and slates, used the Bugsworth Basin, which is being restored. The parish church at Buxworth was built in 1874, and a chapel of ease was provided for Chinley in 1907.

CHURCH BROUGHTON (South Derbyshire)

SK2033: 10 miles (16km) SW of Derby

Isolated in the winding lanes to the south-west of Derby, Church Broughton was formerly part of the Duke of Devonshire's vast Derbyshire estates. It has an impressive **parish church of St Michael**, which mostly dates from the early 14th century. The large west tower, with its Victorian pinnacles and big gargoyles, has a somewhat diminutive spire and a staircase turret, an unusual feature on a Derbyshire church. The long chancel is nearly all from the 14th century, but the tub-shaped font, with its vigorous zigzag patterns, comes from an earlier Norman church.

North of the village stands the hamlet of Barton Blount, with its fine, mainly 18th-century mansion of **Barton Hall**. The stone-encased brick gatehouse to this fine old house dates from the 15th century, when the hall was the home of a famous old soldier, Sir Walter Blount,

the 'Blunt' of Shakespeare's *Henry IV*. The back of the house (which is private) has some handsome, 18th-century, brick chequer-work, and a terrace is decorated by wrought-iron work by Robert Bakewell of Derby.

The **church of St Chad** has tombs to the Bakepuze family, lords of the manor before the Blounts arrived, and it is entered by a fine, 17th-century pedimented doorway.

CHURCH GRESLEY (South Derbyshire)

SK2918: 2 miles (3km) W of Swadlincote

Once at the centre of the South Derbyshire coalfield, Church Gresley and its associated settlement of Castle Gresley seem a little lost, like so many other former mining villages which have had their economic heart torn out. Church Gresley gets its name from the former Austinian priory which was founded here in the early 12th century. Nothing now remains of this or the castle, except for the grassy mound known as Castle Knob and the few bumps and hollows to the east of the present **parish church of St George and St Mary**. The church may also incorporate parts in its lower tower and in a triple-chamfered arch in the east wall. Most of the present church, however, dates from around 1820, and it contains a fine, life-sized alabaster monument to Sir Thomas Gresley, who died in 1699 and lived at nearby Drakelowe Hall.

CLAY CROSS (North East Derbyshire)

SK3963: 5 miles (8km) S of Chesterfield

George Stephenson, inventor of the *Rocket* and resident of Tapton Hall, near Chesterfield, founded the Clay Cross Company in 1837. He had been impressed by the plentiful deposits of coal in the area when he was building the Clay Cross tunnel on the Derby to Chesterfield (North Midland Line) railway, and was determined to exploit them and at the same time supply his new railway. Coal was king in Clay Cross for over a century, but all that is gone today, and this small industrial town to the south of Chesterfield does not have much to recommend it to the visitor.

The **parish church of St Bartholomew**, however, has a graceful broached spire and a dignified interior. It was built by Stevens in 1851, at the height of the town's industrial fame. Windthorpe Hall is a small Elizabethan manor house nearby.

CLOWNE (Bolsover)

SK4975: 9 miles (14km) E of Chesterfield

The unusual name of Clowne has nothing to do with circuses. It comes from the River Poulter, whose old name was the Clun, which rises nearby and flows towards the famous prehistoric site in the craggy Magnesian limestone valley of Creswell Crags. Nearby Markland Grips is another of the peculiar North East Derbyshire 'grips' – an Old English name for a small watercourse. It is now a nature reserve for the Derbyshire Wildlife Trust and has the remains of a promontory enclosure dating from the Iron Age.

Clowne itself is another former mining village, with rows of terraced miners' cottages, on the edge of the parkland of Welbeck Abbey, close to the Nottinghamshire border. The **parish church of St John the Baptist**, on the outskirts of the village, has a battlemented Perpendicular tower and a mostly Norman nave and chancel.

CODNOR (Amber Valley)

SK4149: 2 miles (3km) SE of Ripley

Only the cliff-like ruins remain today of Codnor Castle, the once great baronial home of the Greys and Zouch families, one mile east of the village. The remaining bits of crumbling masonry date from the 13th and 14th centuries and are still impressive, however. They remind the visitor of the days when the great building, consisting of a lower and upper court, stood at the centre of a 1500-acre park. The castle fell into decay when the Zouch family sold the property in 1634. In the park is the 70ft-high (21m) Tuscan column which is a memorial to William Jessop, the celebrated engineer and founder of the famous Butterley Ironworks.

The village itself is distinguished by the pretty **parish church of St James**, with its narrow west tower built to a design by Robert Barker in 1843.

COTON-IN-THE-ELMS (South Derbyshire)

SK2415: 5 miles (8km) S of Burton-on-Trent

According to a recent village history,

50 years ago every road coming into this isolated South Derbyshire village was lined with elms, thus explaining the charming name. Today, of course, the ravages of Dutch Elm Disease have devastated the trees, and the few suckers which spring up soon succumb to the deadly advances of the bark beetle. The last elms to go were three which graced the main street, now filled with mainly modern houses but still watched over by the little **parish church of St Mary.** The church has a graceful tower and spire and was built between 1844 and 46. The original parish church apparently stood behind the Shoulder of Mutton Inn. There is a story that when the church fell into disrepair, the bells were taken to the neighbouring village of Lullington. When the wind is from the south, the villagers of Coton can apparently still hear their old bells ringing out across the intervening fields.

Newton, a self-educated carpenter born at Abney, first became a partner in the mill after the original mill built by Richard Arkwright had burned down in 1785. Newton later became a shining example of the humane treatment of the child apprentices who worked in the mill, in sharp contrast to the deprivations suffered by those employed at Litton Mill, just upstream. Newton built the village school and the charming row of lattice-windowed cottages which face the mill and look down on it from above.

The present mill, with its classical pediment and central cupola with the bell which summoned Newton's apprentices to work, was built in 1815. The 12-bayed building is a sad sight today, having suffered from years of neglect, and is yet another fine old Derbyshire mill in search of a modern use.

CRESSBROOK (Derbyshire Dales)

SK1773: 7 miles (11km) E of Buxton

Tucked away in the steep-sided and winding valley of the River Wye, just upstream from Monsal Head and midway between Bakewell and Buxton, Cressbrook is a little gem of a village. It was largely founded by **William Newton**, the so-called 'Minstrel of the Peak', who was the manager of the magnificent **Cressbrook Mill.** The mill stands at the junction of the Wye with Ravensdale and gives a much better impression of a Georgian country mansion than a cotton manufactory. It is one of Derbyshire's finest monuments of industrial archaeology.

CRESWELL (Bolsover)

SK5274: 11 miles (17km) E of Chesterfield

This former mining village near the Nottinghamshire border is best known for **Creswell Crags**, a beautiful, narrow, lake-filled Magnesian limestone gorge to the east of the village. The crags represent a typical North East Derbyshire 'grip', or narrow valley with a stream running through it. But Creswell Crags are different because they have revealed the most northern evidence of early Man in Europe during the last Ice Age, which ended about 15,000 years ago. In narrow, fissure-type caves like Pin Hole, Mother Grundy's Parlour and Robin Hood's Cave some of the earliest traces of Man in Britain have been excavated. These include little scraps of bone on which the first evidence of Stone Age Man as an artist have been found, with engravings of a horse's head and the stylised figure of a man. The fascinating story of the finds from the Creswell Crag caves is effectively told in the Creswell Crags Visitor Centre at the eastern end of the gorge. Such is the archaeological importance of Creswell Crags that the artefacts of these prehistoric hunter-gatherers have been dignified by the name of the 'Creswellian Culture'. And there are ambitious plans to take the unsightly road out of the gorge, remove the sewage works near the centre, and make it a World Heritage Site, alongside Stonehenge and Hadrian's Wall. The developments at Creswell Crags and on the so-called Robin Hood Line into Nottinghamshire have given a much-needed new lease of life to this once depressed mining village.

CRICH (Derbyshire Dales)

SK3554: 6 miles (10km) SE of Matlock

Pronounced 'crych' this hilltop village over the River Derwent is perhaps best known today for its popular **National Tramway Museum.** The museum occupies the floor of George Stephenson's Crich Cliff Quarry, which served the limekilns alongside the Cromford Canal in the valley floor below. Here trams that once plied the streets of many European cities now ply their trade for visitors, travelling past the reconstructed shop frontages and advertising hoardings of city streets. Above the quarry on **Crich Stand** is the light-

house tower and beacon of the Sherwood Foresters' Memorial (the Nottinghamshire and Derbyshire Regiment), which offers outstanding views as far as the triple towers of Lincoln Cathedral to the east and The Wrekin in the west.

In the village below, the **parish church of St Michael**, is one of the most important in Derbyshire. It has a Norman north arcade and font, a 14th-century chancel and a Perpendicular parapeted west tower. There are fine tombs to the Bellair, Beresford, Claye and Pole families.

CROMFORD (Derbyshire Dales)

SK2956: 2 miles (3km) S of Matlock

The story of Cromford is inextricably linked with that of Richard Arkwright, the semi-literate genius who transformed England from an agricultural nation into the leader of the Industrial Revolution in the latter years of the 18th century. If it had been not situated deep in the Derbyshire hills and access had been a little easier, Cromford could have rivalled Manchester as the cradle of the Industrial Revolution.

Arkwright, a Preston-born wig-maker and barber, came to Cromford in 1771 to use the power of the River Derwent and build the world's first water-powered cotton mill. It is now known as the **Old Mill** and is just off the A6 in Mill Lane. It is another candidate for a Derbyshire World Heritage Site. Now open to the public as a visitor centre, this fortress-like building was designed to deter would-be Luddites who wished to destroy the new machinery which they thought would take work from their traditional cottage industry. **Masson Mill**, on the A6, was built of bright red bricks and with Venetian windows in 1784. Until recently it was still used for textile manufacture. It is currently being renovated.

Between 1782 and 1788, Arkwright built the mock-Gothic **Willersley Castle** just over Cromford's famous 15th-century bridge across the Derwent, complete with its rare bridge chapel and 18th-century Fishing Pavilion. Unfortunately, he didn't live to enjoy it for long as he died in 1792.

Below Willersley Castle stands the **parish church of St Mary**, built on the orders of Arkwright in 1797. It is mainly in the Perpendicular style and contains the tomb of the man who put Cromford so firmly on the map.

But Arkwright did much more than just bring industry to the valley of the Derwent at Cromford. He also provided for the welfare of his employees in a way never seen before in Britain. He built good quality accommodation for them, such as the fine, three-storeyed, stone-built terraces in North Street, and a village school in the main part of the village, west of the A6, across the limestone cutting known as **Scarthin Nick**. And in Greyhound Square, he provided the grand façade of the Greyhound Inn, as somewhere for his workers' recreation after work. Behind Greyhound Square is Cromford's millpond, known as The Dam, a tranquil spot away from the rushing traffic. Another famous name connected with Cromford is the children's author, **Alison Uttley** (1884-1976), who was born at Castle Top Farm, where she lived until her late teens. Village life in Cromford in the late 19th century is recalled in her books *The Farm on the Hill*, and *The Country Child*, although she is perhaps best known for her 'Little Grey Rabbit' and 'Sam Pig' stories.

Alongside the river is the restored Cromford Canal, which linked with the ambitious Cromford and High Peak Railway (now the High Peak Trail). The railway had been completed in 1831 and crossed the high White Peak plateau to Whaley Bridge, at the beginning of the Railway Age. Both canal and former railway are now enjoyed by leisure users.

CUBLEY (Derbyshire Dales)

SK1637: 5 miles (8km) S of Ashbourne

Lying on the old Roman road known as Long Lane in the green countryside to the south of Ashbourne, Cubley has a long and distinguished history. Its **parish church of St Andrew** is on the site of one mentioned in the Domesday Book. The present structure has a fine Perpendicular tower, and most of the chancel inside dates from the 13th century. Despite its age, it is a light and airy church because of the large west window and late 17th-century windows in the nave. There are many memorials to the Montgomery family; particularly impressive is the alabaster tomb chest to Sir Nicholas Montgomery, who died in 1494. There are traces of medieval wall paintings on the chancel arch and in the east nave arcade. Cubley was the birthplace of Samuel Johnson's father, who became a Lichfield bookseller and gave the world the first great lexicographer.

A mile to the east along the Alkmonton road is **Bentley Hall**, which dates from the Elizabethan and Jacobean periods, and looks a little like a miniature Sudbury Hall. It is built of brick with stone quoins, and has a central bay window supported by stone pillars on the first floor of the east wing. It is now a private farmhouse.

CURBAR (Derbyshire Dales)

SK2574: 5 miles (8km) NW of Bakewell

Although it never gets the same publicity, Curbar had an equally tragic 'visitation' of the plague some thirty-three years before it reached the more famous 'Plague Village' of Eyam, across the River Derwent. Evidence of this is provided by the collection of simple stone slabs beneath **Curbar Edge**, the gritstone escarpment which dominates the eastern side of the hillside village. Dated 1632, they mark the graves of the Cundy family and a man called Sheldon. There are other pitiful reminders of plague victims just below the Wesleyan Reform Chapel, which was built in 1862 from stone quarried from a nearby field.

Curbar today is very much a commuter village for Sheffield and Chesterfield. Its small **parish church of All Saints** was built in 1868. There is a circular, conical-roofed village lock-up at the top end of the village, south of the main village street.

Stoke Hall, about two miles to the north-west of the village, is a stately, two and a half-storeyed, stone-built mansion with a fine Tuscan columned doorway, built in 1757. **Cliffe College**, on the outskirts of the village, is a modern Methodist training and conference

centre. At the end of the last century, missionaries were trained here.

DALE ABBEY (Erewash)

SK4338: 6 miles (10km) NE of Derby

A gaunt, empty chancel window standing forlornly in a grassy field is all that remains of the abbey which gave the village its name. Dale Abbey's once great Premonstratensian house was founded in around 1160 and dissolved in 1538. A small museum in what remains of the chapter house tells the story.

Just across the valley and carved out of the sandstone cliffs is the **Hermitage**, which was built by a 12th-century Derby baker named Cornelius, who had a vision to come to Depedale, as Dale Abbey was then known, to live as a recluse. His cave is well preserved and has a doorway and two windows. When Cornelius discovered a water supply nearby, it also became a place of pilgrimage.

All Saints Parish Church, which measures 26ft by 25ft (7m by 8m), is one of the smallest and strangest in the country. It shares its roof with an adjoining farmhouse, which was rebuilt on the site in 1883. The interior is crammed tightly with box pews. There is also a gallery and, to the left of the altar, a pulpit which dates from 1634. The masonry of the tiny nave is Norman in date, and the church may represent what remains of the chapel of Depedale, which is mentioned in the late 12th century. All Saints was a 'peculiar' church, at which couples could be married without their banns being read.

The 18th-century **Cat and Fiddle Windmill** is the only one of its kind left in Derbyshire, and stands on the site of an even earlier mill.

DARLEY DALE
(Derbyshire Dales)

SK2763: 2 miles (3km) north of Matlock

Motorists heading north from Derby on the A6, towards the Peak District, don't see the best of Darley Dale. To them it appears to be a one-street village of rather dull, Victorian terraced cottages, with the grand Gothic **Whitworth Institute** standing at one end. This is a legacy of the village's most famous benefactor, Sir Joseph Whitworth (1803-87), the great Victorian engineer and inventor of the Whitworth screw thread.

The old, original part of the village lies to the west, closer to the River Derwent. It clusters protectively around the wonderful **parish church of St Helen**, which in turn is protected by Darley Dale's famous and massive **yew tree**. Estimates of the yew's age range from 600 to 4000 years, and the stone tablets which surround its enormous, gnarled old trunk – 33ft (10m) in circumference – record moments in history which it has lived through. The church itself is of a cruciform shape and dates mainly from the 13th and 14th centuries, but there is evidence of a much earlier establishment. There are 12th- and 13th-century sepulchral stones built into the walls, and the shaft of a highly decorated Saxon cross. Following a 19th-century restoration, some fine and colourful stained glass in the Arts and Crafts style by Sir Edward Burne-Jones

and Ford Madox Brown was inserted in the south transept.

Sir Joseph Whitworth – motto 'Let us Try' – is buried in the church. This inventive Stockport-born engineer gave much to his adopted village. He lived at **Stancliffe Hall**, which was designed by E.M. Barrie and is now a school. Nearby is the Stancliffe Quarry, which has provided gritstone blocks for, among other projects, the Thames Embankment and Hyde Park Corner in London, and the Walker Art Gallery in Liverpool. Mention has already been made of the **Whitworth Institute**, which originally contained a library, recreation room, gymnasium, swimming pool and a museum. It is still a well-used community centre for the modern villagers. Whitworth also provided the Whitworth Hospital and the

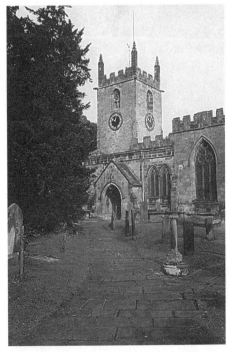

The Parish Church of St Helen, Darley Dale, with ancient yew tree on the left.

Whitworth Park, for what he hoped would be a model village, but despite his generosity, he was apparently unpopular with villagers.

Just outside the village, near the hamlet of Two Dales, stands **The Holt**, an elegant, three-bay Georgian house. It has a Saxon cross shaft that is decorated with interlace patterns and possibly dates from the 11th century. On **Oaker Hill** above, there is a solitary sycamore which found its way into a sonnet by William Wordsworth. The story is that when two local brothers left the village to seek their fortune they each planted a tree. One of the brothers never returned, so only one tree survives.

DENBY (Amber Valley)

SK3946: 10 miles (16km) N of Derby

Denby, first recorded in the Domesday Book as 'Denebi', is probably best known today for its distinctive pottery and stoneware, which is exported all over the world. The story of how it came by chance to this former coal and iron village goes back to when the Denby to Alfreton turnpike was being constructed in 1806. By chance, a bed of clay was uncovered which proved to be ideal for the making of stoneware. As a result, the Denby Pottery was started in 1809, and still flourishes, with a 'seconds shop' and visitor centre, today.

Denby's **parish church of St Mary** has a broach spire, a stone-vaulted south porch and a probably 13th-century south arcade. A gallery took the place of the north arcade in the 19th century.

Denby Old Hall (private), to the west

of the church, is a two-gabled farmhouse dating from the 16th and 17th centuries, with Elizabethan mullioned windows. Denby was granted the right to hold a market and a two-day fair in 1334. But the only remnant of this honour is the church flower festival held annually in September. Among Denby's most famous sons is John Flamsteed, the first Astronomer Royal. He was born here in 1646 and started his great career at the Royal Observatory at Greenwich on the princely salary of £100 a year.

DERBY (Derby)

SK3435: 15 miles (24km) W of Nottingham

The great city of Derby has undergone several changes of name in its 2000-year history. The first recorded settlement was the Roman fort of Derventio, built around AD48 on the banks of, and taking its name from, the River Derwent. The place is now marked by a green, known as Little Chesters, north of St Mary's Bridge (with its rare 15th-century chapel). The Saxons settled in the area in the fifth century and built a new village nearby, which they named Northworthy, meaning 'the northern enclosure'. It was near the modern St Alkmund's Way. The next invaders were the Danes, some 300 years later, and they renamed the village Derby, which probably means 'the farm of the animals or deer'. It soon became one of the five major boroughs in their Danelaw. The new name was first recorded in 917, when the borough was invaded by the Mercian queen, Aethelflaeda. Eventually, Danes and Saxons were united under Cnut, and they lived peacefully together until the coming of the Normans in 1066, when the area was laid waste like so much of the north. It later became a prosperous trading town in the Middle Ages, receiving its first market charter from Henry II in 1154, and another from King John in 1204.

Today, Derby is regarded as a major industrial city. The process of industrialisation began when John Lombe and George Sorocold built their Silk Mill, the first in England, on the Derwent in 1717. Today the historic mill has become the **Industrial Museum**, telling the story of the city's rise to national power and importance with a series of lively displays and galleries. But it was the coming of the railway in 1840 which really put Derby on the map, transforming it from a minor provincial town into one of the great industrial cities of England. It has been called the city of the Transport Age. Certainly, its emergence as a great railway terminus on the Midland and Great Northern lines, with the associated railway works, and the establishment of the prestigious and internationally famous Rolls-Royce car and aero-engine works in 1907, have put Derby at the forefront of this field.

Derby's stately **Cathedral of All Saints** was not raised to that status until 1927, and the town itself did not become a city until 1977. It has now emerged, after years of grimy Victorian mediocrity, to become one of the liveliest cities in the East Midlands. The cathedral boasts one of the tallest and most magnificent medieval towers in the country, and it has been a prominent, 212ft (65m) landmark in Derby since it was built in the early years of the 16th century. The rest of the cathedral was completely rebuilt in 1723-25 by James Gibbs, who made All Saints one of the finest 18th-century town churches in the country. From the outside, it looks almost like two churches, with the soaring Gothic splendour of the tower contrasting sharply with the rusticated Georgian windows and low balustrades of the 18th-century work. In the interior, the Tuscan columns and sweeping plaster vault have an impressive counterpoint in local man Robert Bakewell's ornate, wrought-iron chancel screen, described by Pevsner as the most important possession of the cathedral. There are fine monuments, especially to the Cavendish family, including the tomb of Elizabeth, Countess of Shrewsbury, better known as Bess of Hardwick, (1607); Caroline Cavendish, Countess of Bessborough (1760); and Richard Bateman (1821) – the latter by Francis Chantrey.

Today, the cathedral stands aloof above the constant roar of Derby's infamous inner ring road traffic, which dips beneath an underpass almost beneath the tower. There are several fine Georgian houses in nearby St Mary's Gate, including the County Hall, which dates from 1660 and is a fine, five-bayed building with tall, arched windows. Also in St Mary's Gate is Derby's newest attraction, the **Police Museum**. This street leads through Cheapside to Wardwick (first recorded in Saxon times as 'Walda's Wick' or 'dairy farm'), where the 17th-century, twin-gabled Jacobean Café stands opposite the Flemish Gothic-style **Library and Museum**, built in 1878. At the rear of this is the **Art Gallery**

(1883) and Robert Bakewell's iron gates to the **Silk Mill Industrial Museum**.

Friargate is one of the finest Georgian streets in Britain, and certainly the best in Derby. Nearly all the houses are mid-Georgian in date and reward a leisurely stroll to examine their classical details. Close to the wonderfully ornate **Cast Iron Bridges**, made by Andrew Handyside in 1848 to allow the Great Northern Railway to span the street, is Number 42, with its five-bay façade of red bricks. Now known as Pickford's House, it has been tastefully restored to a living museum which allows the visitor to appreciate what life was like for the original owner, architect Joseph Pickford, in 1770.

Derby's central **Market Place** has several fine old buildings, including the Greek-influenced Town Hall, with its tall central tower and domed top. The town hall was built in 1841, the market hall behind in 1864, and the modernised Assembly Rooms were originally built in 1763-74.

Derby's other claim to international fame is for its porcelain. The first porcelain factory was established in the 1740s and was one of the earliest in Britain. Its founder was probably Andrew Planche, son of a Huguenot immigrant. Some of this earliest work is on display in the ceramics gallery of the museum. Visitors are welcome at the modern **Royal Crown Derby Factory** in Osmaston Road. The factory was founded in King Street in 1875, and awarded the Royal Warrant in 1890.

Derby has over twenty fine parks, the oldest of which is the Arboretum. This was given to the town by Joseph Strutt and contains a monument to Sir Henry

Royce, the founder of the Rolls-Royce Company, which has been associated with Derby since 1907.

The most recent new development in Derby is Pride Park, a shopping and leisure centre on the outskirts of the city, and now the splendid new home of Derby County Football Club – the Premiership football club which takes as its nickname the county's famous mascot, the Derby Ram.

DETHICK (Amber Valley)

SK3257: 4 miles (6km) SE of Matlock

Standing on the hills high above the valley of the River Derwent, Dethick occupies a breezy situation with lovely views, especially towards the west. Its most famous son was Sir Anthony Babington, a prominent Tudor Roman Catholic who plotted the death of Queen Elizabeth and the release of Mary Queen of Scots, then being held prisoner at nearby Wingfield Manor. He was later hanged, drawn and quartered for his treachery. Nothing remains of Babington's Manor House, but the large stone-built barn on the site dates from that period. Babington was responsible for the building of the lavish and elaborate west tower of the **chapel of St John the Baptist**, built in 1539. It is decorated with an array of coats of arms which show the descendancy of the Babington family. The Babingtons came to Dethick as a result of Thomas Babington, who fought at Agincourt, marrying the heiress of the Dethick family. Most of the rest of the chapel is 13th century, with two fine lancet windows and a 16th-century clerestory. The **parish church of**

Christ Church is Victorian Perpendicular in style and was built in 1901-3.

Nearby are the hamlets of **Lea** and **Lea Bridge**, where the famous knitwear firm of John Smedley occupies a former cotton mill originally built by Peter Nightingale in 1784, and later seeing service as a hat factory. John Marsden Smedley, the founder of the company, lived at Lea Green and was a notable local landowner and benefactor. He built houses for his workers, and one of the first factory hospitals in the country in some neighbouring buildings, which are now known as the Post Office Cottages. The early Georgian mansion of Lea Hall is on the site of a 14th-century manor house.

DINTING (High Peak)

SK0294: 1 mile (2km) W of Glossop

The most impressive feature of this small village west of Glossop, on the main road to Manchester, is the towering, 120ft (36m) high **Dinting Viaduct** which carries the main Sheffield to Manchester railway line. The line was opened in 1845 as the Sheffield, Ashton and Manchester Railway, and passes through the infamous three-mile long Woodhead Tunnel at the head of nearby Longdendale.

Dinting's **Holy Trinity Parish Church** has a graceful, tall spire and was built in the Victorian Gothic style in 1875. But all in Dinting is dwarfed by that massive viaduct, a monument to the Railway Age.

DOVE HOLES (High Peak)

SK0778: 3 miles (5km) N of Buxton

Anywhere less like the more famous Dove Holes in Dovedale would be hard to imagine, but the village post office still regularly has visitors looking for the famous limestone dale. This bleak, one-street village, high on what used to be the moors north of Buxton, is surrounded by quarries and lime works and always seems to wear an air of desolation. The small Victorian Gothic **parish church**, the chapel and rows of quarrymen's cottages line up along the A6 as it heads between Buxton and Chapel-en-le-Frith, and there's not much to tempt the traveller to stop. The **Bull Ring Henge** monument, just to the east of the village, behind the church, dates from the Late Neolithic period, so is of the same period and about the same size as the better-known Arbor Low. But even this feature had its standing stones removed in the 18th century for building material, and it now stands rather forlorn, surrounded by quarry waste tips.

DOVERIDGE (Derbyshire Dales)

SK1134: 2 miles (3km) E of Uttoxeter

The dedication of the **parish church to St Cuthbert** is unusual in Derbyshire. This delightful, mainly 13th-century building once stood in the grounds of Doveridge Hall, which has since been demolished. The former parkland of the old hall, which was built in 1769 for Sir Henry Cavendish, is now filled with new houses and many of the residents commute to Derby, Burton or Uttoxeter, just across the border in Staffordshire.

The graceful lancet windows in the chancel and the priest's doorway in the church are said to be among the finest examples of 13th-century Early English work in the county. They are watched over by an embattled tower of the same period. There are memorials to the Cavendishes and the Royalist Sir Thomas Milward in the church. It is approached through a tunnel of branches formed by Doveridge's ancient yew, which could be 1200 years old, and certainly predates the church. Local legend says that Robin Hood was betrothed to Maid Marion under its branches.

The village name comes from the Old English and means 'the bridge over the River Dove'. There are two bridges now, a modern one which takes the roaring traffic of the A50, and the original six-arched medieval one, now mercifully closed to traffic. The Dove here marks the boundary between Derbyshire and Staffordshire.

DRAYCOTT (Erewash)

SK4433: 5 miles (8km) SE of Derby

The original settlement here, in the low-lying water-meadows where the River Derwent ends its 60-mile journey through Derbyshire and joins the Trent, was at **Wilne**, an appropriate name which means 'a clearing in the willows'. And it was here that the first **parish church of St Chad** was recorded in 822. The present church, a mile south of Draycott in the water-meadows and stranded between flooded sand and gravel pits, dates from the 13th and 14th centuries, and is one of the finest in the county. All that remains from the Saxon church is the font, which was made from part of a circular Saxon cross with carvings of dragons and birds. Espe-

cially memorable inside the church is the Willoughby Chapel, built in 1622 for the Willoughbys of Risley (see RISLEY), for whom Wilne was the original parish church. Inside is the great alabaster wall monument to Sir John Willoughby, who died in 1622, and another to Ann Willoughby, who died in 1688. Unexpected rarities in the chapel are the pretty and brightly coloured 17th-century floor tiles and original stained glass windows, which are probably Flemish. The church was gutted by fire in 1917 and reopened, after a tasteful restoration, in 1923. Only two houses and the old corn mill remain of the original settlement of Wilne, although the church still serves Draycott parish. The settlement moved up to Draycott (or 'dry cote') – no doubt because of the frequent flooding of the river.

The major building in the village is the **Victoria Lace Mill** which, when completed in 1907, was said to be the largest manufacturing mill in Europe, having the same dimensions as Noah's Ark. The clock tower of the mill is a landmark for miles around.

DRONFIELD (North East Derbyshire)

SK3578: 5 miles (8km) N of Chesterfield

Situated midway between Chesterfield and Sheffield, Dronfield is thankfully bypassed by the A61. The old market town still clings to the western side of the valley of the River Drone, as it has for hundreds of years. Under the recent Boundaries Commission review, there were proposals to merge Dronfield with Sheffield, but fierce local opposition ensured that it stayed where it had always been: in Derbyshire.

Dronfield has expanded rapidly in the last thirty years as a commuter town for Chesterfield and Sheffield, but the centre of the old town has retained its 18th-century charm. There are a number of fine Georgian houses in the High Street, notably the early 18th-century Manor House, which now serves as the council offices, and the former Grammar School Headmaster's House, dated 1731.

At the centre of the town, at the top of the High Street, is the **Peel Monument**, erected to celebrate the repeal of the Corn Laws in 1848. The market cross formerly stood on this site. Although the market was recently revived, Dronfield's original market, for which Charles II granted a charter in 1662, always suffered from the proximity of Sheffield and Chesterfield. Close to the Monument in the High Street is a house known as The Cottage, which is believed to have been owned by Lord Byron.

The **parish church of St John the Baptist**, with its 14th-century chancel and fine Perpendicular tower and spire overlooking the town, has some fine woodwork inside, including poppyheaded stalls and a Jacobean pulpit.

Meadows; and the delightful little Baptist Chapel, whose brick front dates from 1830, and which has a house attached to it. **Duffield Hall**, at the southern entrance to the village, was originally Elizabethan, but the house was enlarged in 1870 and became a Roman Catholic girls' school. Today, it is the imposing headquarters of the Derbyshire Building Society.

Only the mound of Castle Hill remains of **Duffield Castle**, which was one of the most formidable Norman fortresses in England. It was erected by Henry of the powerful de Ferrers family. When the site was excavated in 1886, the foundations of the keep proved it to be one of the largest in Britain. It was nearly 100ft (30m) square and had walls 16ft (5m) thick.

The **parish church of St Alkmund** stands apart to the south of the village, in the water-meadows of the River Derwent. It has an elegant 14th-century tower and recessed spire, with a beautiful, five-light, Perpendicular east window in the chancel. There is an extraordinary wall monument with an acrostic inscription to Anthony Bradshaw, who died in 1614, his two wives and 20 children. Bradshaw was a barrister and deputy steward of Duffield Frith, a former hunting forest between Duffield and Wirksworth.

DUFFIELD (Amber Valley)

SK3443: 5 miles (8km) N of Derby

Duffield is one of the finest small towns in Derbyshire, with a lovely mixture of buildings in its main street, including some particularly fine Georgian houses. These include the The Ferns, a three-bayed, brick-built house; The

EARL STERNDALE (High Peak)

SK0967: 5 miles (8km) S of Buxton

Situated close to the spectacular reef limestone peaks of High Wheeldon, Hitter Hill and Chrome and Parkhouse Hills at the less-frequented, northern end of the Dove Valley, Earl Sterndale is one of the hidden gems of the Peak District. It stands over 1100ft (335m) above the sea and is surrounded by a number of farms called 'granges' – a reminder that during the Middle Ages much of this land was owned by Basingwerk Abbey. Earl Sterndale's usual claim to fame in the guidebooks is its pub, the 400-year-old **Quiet Woman** in the main village street. The sign shows a headless woman with the caption: 'Soft words turneth away wrath.' It is said to illustrate the sad fate of a former landlord's wife who talked too much. The pub was in the hands of the Heathcote family, still a common local surname, for nearly 300 years.

The small, early 19th-century **parish church of St Michael** has the unusual distinction of being the only church in Derbyshire to suffer a direct hit from a bomb during the Second World War. It was restored and refurbished in 1952, but retains its Saxon font.

ECKINGTON (North East Derbyshire)

SK4379: 7 miles (11km) NE of Chesterfield

Eckington is a former colliery village, but like so many others in this part of north-east Derbyshire, the pits are long gone and the long, sprawling village – the main street is over a mile long – has become the home for many workers in Sheffield and Chesterfield. It has a Saxon origin, and the **parish church of St Peter and St Paul** is described by Pevsner as being 'of exceptional architectural interest' because of the outstanding 12th- and 13th-century work.

The big, square tower dominates the eastern end of the village, near to where the River Moss enters the Rother, and features a splendid western doorway with Early English details. The spire dates from the 14th century, but the rather plain exterior of the church gives nothing away about the splendours of the inside. Here the five impressively tall bays of the nave arcades are held up by circular piers which may date from as early as the 12th century. And to top it all, there is a splendid Perpendicular-style clerestory. There are monuments to the Sitwell family of nearby Renishaw Hall, and a Spanish altar painting bought here by Sir Sitwell Sitwell.

Renishaw Hall, on the south-eastern outskirts of the village, has been the home of the Sitwell family since 1625, when George Sitwell built the first house. This was incorporated in the present rambling, mainly Jacobean mansion by Sitwell Sitwell around 1800. Renishaw has links with all the famous Sitwell authors, including Edith, Osbert and Sacheverell, the father of the present owner of the house. Today the parkland surrounding the house is a golf course, but the house, including the vineyard created in 1972, is open to the public.

EDALE (High Peak)

SK1285: 5 miles NE of Chapel-en-le-Frith

Edale is a very popular centre for Peak District walkers, situated at the southern edge of the **Kinder Scout plateau**, which at 2088ft (636m) is the highest point in the county. It is perhaps best known by walkers as the starting point of Tom Stephenson's classic long-distance path, the **Pennine Way**,

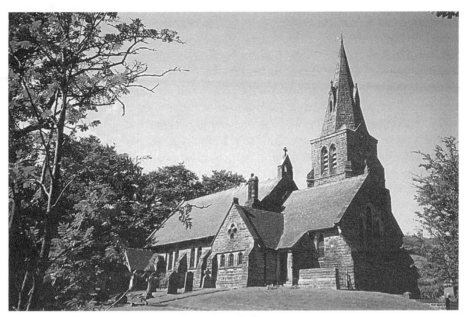

Edale Parish Church

which sets off on its 270-mile route to Kirk Yetholm, just across the Scottish Border, from the famous Log Bridge north of Edale village.

Edale is actually made up of five quite separate farming hamlets, each of which has the suffix 'booth' – a Tudor word meaning 'a temporary shelter for herdsmen'. From the east, the Edale booths are Nether Booth, Ollerbrook Booth, Grindsbrook Booth, Barber Booth and Upper Booth, although the name of Edale Village is usually given to the largest of these, Grindsbrook Booth. Here is where the Sheffield to Stockport railway line, built in 1894, has its station – on a scenic route still known as the 'Ramblers' Route'. And it is here that the charming little Victorian **parish church**, built in 1886 and the third on the site, is situated, along with the village school and post office. The Peak District National Park's Field-head Visitor Centre is also here, along with the 300-year-old **Nag's Head Inn**,

where the Pennine Way officially starts. **Edale Mill**, just down the valley to the east, was originally built as a cotton mill and now provides holiday accommodation. Much of the surrounding moorland, including most of Kinder Scout, is now in the hands of the National Trust, but livestock farming, particularly sheep, is still the main enterprise in the five Edale booths.

EDENSOR (Derbyshire Dales)

SK2469: 2 miles (3km) NE of Bakewell

Edensor (pronounced 'Ensor') is Chatsworth House's village, a pretty little estate village built in 1839 by the 6th Duke of Devonshire. He 'transplanted' the original Domesday Book village of the same name lock, stock and barrel to this site, because it was apparently spoiling the view from the great house. With the help of his brilliant gardener, Joseph Paxton, and his architect, John Robertson of Derby, he choose to build every house with completely different design details, from Swiss chalet to Tudor cottage, so that no two in this model village are exactly the same. The whole effect is surprisingly pleasing, and the village is watched over by the graceful spire of the **parish church of St Peter**, built in 1867 to the design of Sir George Gilbert Scott. Inside are monuments to the Cavendish family, and in the churchyard is the ducal burial ground where lies, among others, Kathleen Kennedy. She was the sister of President John Kennedy and died in an air crash soon after her husband, Lord Hartington, the present Duke's brother, had been killed in the Second World War. Also buried in the churchyard is Paxton, the creator of the village, who went on to design London's Crystal Palace.

But Edensor is overshadowed by the Big House across the manicured parklands and River Derwent. Most of the present **Chatsworth House** dates from the rebuilding by the 4th Earl between 1678 and 1707, which was completed by the 1st Duke. The well-known west front, reflected in the waters of the River Derwent, is in the classical Palladian style, and is so well recognised that it now serves as the Chatsworth logo.

Known for good reason as 'the Palace of the Peak', Chatsworth is not so much a stately home as a treasure house of priceless works of art, collected by the Cavendish family from all over the world. A day is not really long enough to take in all of Chatsworth's riches, but first-time visitors should not miss the magnificent, recently refurbished Painted Hall, with its wonderful, late 17th century, allegorical painted ceilings and walls by Louis Laguerre; the sumptuous State Dining, Drawing and Music Rooms; and the wonderfully light and airy Sculpture Gallery, with its superb marble statuary. The Great Dining Room has also been recently and very tastefully refurbished in typical Chatsworth style. Yet despite all this opulence, Chatsworth still manages to retain its atmosphere of a family home, and the present Duke and Duchess still take an active part in running the estate and house, once described by the Duchess as, 'Not so much a house as a town.' The Duchess has taken a particularly active role in promoting the business side of the estate, promoting the Farm Shop in the nearby estate village of **Pilsley**. Finally, Chatsworth's wonderful gardens are worth a visit in their own right. They range from formal planned beds and the magnificent Emperor Fountain to the recently restored Maze and the informal Woodland Walks in the Stand Woods above the house. The Old Deer Park is home to Chatsworth's fine herds of red and fallow deer, and the Children's Farmyard is another more recent attraction in the grounds behind the house.

EGGINTON (South Derbyshire)

SK2628: 3 miles (5km) NW of Burton-upon-Trent

Seldom visited by the roaring traffic half a mile (1km) to the west as it speeds along on the A38 between Derby and Burton, Egginton lies on the River Dove in peaceful tranquillity. Like so many other south Derbyshire villages, Egginton is very much a commuter village for the nearby towns of Derby and Burton-upon-Trent.

Monks Bridge across the Dove was perhaps first built by and takes its name from the monks of Tutbury Priory, but it was widened to its present four segmented arches in 1775. Mercifully, it is now bypassed by a modern concrete one which carries the A38. Nearby, the **Trent and Mersey Canal** is carried over the Dove on the long, nine-arched aqueduct built to the design of James Brindley in 1777.

In ancient times, Egginton was the home of the Every family, whose family seat of Egginton Hall, originally a fine Tudor hall, but rebuilt in Georgian red brick in 1780, was sadly demolished in 1954. Now only the ruins of the stables can be seen in a sea of modern development.

Another reminder of the old lords of the manor is the Every Arms, a former coaching inn which is a landmark on the A38 dual carriageway. Egginton had its brief moment of fame in 1644, when a Royalist force was defeated by Cromwell's forces in the Battle of Egginton Heath.

The low-towered **parish church of St Wilfrid** is mainly 13th century with some dark, 15th-century stained glass.

ELMTON (Bolsover)

SK5073: 3 miles (5km) NW of Bolsover

Sadly, the elms which gave Elmton its name have long gone, and this small rural village in the middle of the north Derbyshire coalfield now lies quietly in the arable fields between Bolsover and Creswell. The **parish church of St Peter** was entirely rebuilt in the Georgian style in 1773, but the western tower was never finished and gives it a strangely truncated appearance. An unusual feature inside this simple little church is the tester – or sounding board – above the pulpit. Elmton's most famous son, remembered by a portrait in the vestry, was Jedediah Buxton, an illiterate farm labourer who was, nevertheless, a mathematical genius. Born the son of the village schoolmaster in 1707, he achieved a brief period of national fame and was 'exhibited' in London at the Royal Society. He returned home and died in 1772, and was buried in the churchyard of St Peter's.

ELTON (Derbyshire Dales)

SK2261: 5 miles (8km) S of Bakewell

Elton lies high on the White Peak limestone plateau, surrounded by the remains of centuries of lead mining, which are revealed in the numerous bumps and hollows in its fields. Many of the good limestone cottages in the village street date from the heyday of the lead mining industry in the 18th century, when most of the occupants were engaged in the dual economy of mining and farming. **Elton Hall**, which has a date stone of 1668 in a semicircular pediment above the door, is now the Youth Hostel, and the village has become a popular centre for walking in the White Peak.

The **parish church of All Saints** stands in the centre of the village and was completely rebuilt in 1812, after the old steeple collapsed on the previous medieval church. There is an interesting story connected to the font, which is a copy of the original 12th-century Norman one. The villagers, not realising its worth, allowed the original to go to nearby Youlgreave. Here it was recognised for its antiquity and was 're-scued' from the vicarage garden to occupy pride of place in Youlgreave parish church.

ELVASTON (South Derbyshire)

SK4132: 5 miles (8km) SE of Derby

Elvaston now forms part of the suburban sprawl to the south of Derby, along with Alvaston, Spondon and Borrowash. It is perhaps best known for stately **Elvaston Castle**, at the centre of one of the first country park to be opened in the country, in 1969. A partnership between Derbyshire County Council and Derby City Council secured the future of the castle and its continued use as a valuable recreational open space for the people of this part of the county. The building is also now the headquarters of the Derbyshire Wildlife Trust. The property came into the possession of the Stanhope family, later the Earls of Harrington, in 1539. They retained it until 1964.

The present castle, a battlemented structure, was designed by James Wyatt in 1812, although the east front is by Lewis Cottingham. The famous Painted Hall is by Robert Walker, who added the stucco wings and tower to the west front. The greatest glories of Elvaston, however, are its formal gardens, grottoes, a Moorish temple and yew topiaries. These were all laid out by the 4th Earl of Harrington and are approached by the famous Golden Gates to the south. These elaborate, blue and gold, cast-iron structures are

reputed to have been taken from Madrid by Napoleon, and acquired by the Earl as 'spoils of war'. Cricket has been played on the adjacent pitch for 150 years.

Close to the castle is the interesting **parish church of St Bartholomew,** with its unusual three-storeyed and pinnacled west tower. Most of the rest of the church belongs to the 13th and 14th centuries. It contains many splendid monuments to the Stanhopes and the Earls of Harrington.

Interesting buildings in the rest of the village include the Village Hall, formerly the village school built in 1852, and the Clockhouse, a three-storeyed building built as a 'Refuge for the Aged Poor' ten years later, and now a retirement home. The Harrington Arms in nearby Thulston was the scene of a Mummers or Guisers Play enacted every Christmas. The former vicarage, **Thurlaston Grange**, is an attractive listed building dating from the Georgian period.

ETWALL (South Derbyshire)

SK2732: 5 miles (8km) SW of Derby

This small village to the south-west of Derby is overshadowed by the massive John Port Comprehensive School, which serves over 1700 pupils who are bussed in from the surrounding villages. The school was built on the site of the former Etwall Hall, an early 18th-century, five-bayed manor house which was the home of the Port family. The family's most famous son, Sir John Port, was the founder of Repton School. The hall's beautiful wrought-iron gates were made by Robert Bakewell of Derby. They were saved when the hall was demolished and now grace the entrance to the charming open courtyard of the almshouses, which were founded by Sir John Port and re-built in 1681. These pleasant houses were recently refurbished to provide accommodation for retired local people. To the south-east lies the giant Toyota car factory, at which many local people are employed.

Etwall gets its name from the Old English 'Eata's stream' and the Etwall Brook runs through the village. **St Helen's Parish Church** lies between the village street and the almshouses, and although it looks mainly Perpendicular from the outside, inside there is evidence of much earlier, Norman work. The north aisle forms the chapel of the Hospital, as the almshouses were once known, and there are memorials to members of the Port family, including the grand, canopied tomb of Sir John Port, who died in 1541, with brasses of Port and his wife and children.

EYAM (Derbyshire Dales)

SK2176: 5 miles (8km) N of Bakewell

Eyam (pronounced 'Eem') cannot escape its slightly morbid past, and it seems it will forever be saddled with the epithet – 'The Plague Village'. Not that the epic story of the self-imposed sacrifice which the villagers made during the plague years of 1665-66 should ever be forgotten. Led by their minister, the Reverend William Mompesson and his Nonconformist predecessor, the Reverend Thomas Stanley, the villagers imposed a quarantine so that the deadly virus would not spread through the rest of the county. The result was that around 350 villagers died over the two years, and the names of the victims can still be seen on their cottages throughout the hillside village. Some of their pitiful graves can also be seen in the fields around the village, because they were not allowed to be buried in the churchyard during the 'visitation'.

Eyam Hall

Church services were also held in the open air to minimise the risk of infection, at the little limestone crag of **Cucklett Delf** below the village. Modern critics have questioned whether the fatal outbreak was, in fact, the plague, as an epidemic of any disease was known as the plague in those days. And they have also challenged the wisdom of the self-imposed quarantine, which resulted in far more deaths. Whatever the facts, medical knowledge was scarce in 17th-century Derbyshire, and the villagers undoubtedly took their brave action from the highest possible motives. The **Eyam Museum** in the former Methodist Chapel in Hawkhill Road has award-winning exhibits and displays which graphically tell the harrowing story of the Eyam Plague.

The restored 13th-century **parish church of St Lawrence** has many touching memorials of the plague, including a book of the victims, William Mompesson's chair, and the table-top tomb of his wife, Catherine. This can be found in the churchyard, close to the magnificent, though truncated, **Saxon cross**. Among the other features in this fascinating church are the medieval wall paintings, much good Jacobean woodwork, and an elaborate 18th-century sundial over the south door.

Close to the church, opposite the village green and the stocks, is the late 17th-century **Eyam Hall**, a lovely gabled and mullioned building which has been the home of the Wright family ever since it was built in 1676. Recently opened to the public for the first time, Eyam Hall is a wonderfully intimate and lived-in house, with some exceptionally fine tapestries upstairs and a new herb garden at the rear. There is also a craft centre with shops and a buttery-type restaurant in the stables at the back of the building.

Despite its grisly past, Eyam is a lively village, and the Victorian Village Institute opposite the church is still the centre for most social activities. The **Eyam well-dressings** are among the last but most accomplished of the season, held during late August and early September.

FENNY BENTLEY (Derbyshire Dales)

SK1750: 2 miles (3km) N of Ashbourne

Bisected by the busy A515 Ashbourne-Buxton road, Fenny Bentley is often overlooked by the tourists rushing on to the next Peak District 'honeypot'. But this pretty little village on the Bentley Brook rewards a longer look. The most important building in the village apart from the **parish church of St Edmund** is Cherry Orchard Farm (private), once known as Bentley Hall. The squat, medieval defensive tower of the hall looks more like a Northumbrian pele tower than anything else, and dates from the late 15th century when the building was the seat of the Beresford family. A fine, gabled and mullioned farmhouse is attached to the tower.

Sir Thomas Beresford fought with one of his sons alongside Henry V at Agincourt, and is buried in a grand alabaster tomb in the church. It is said that every Beresford is descended from this family, and until recently an annual convention of people with that surname was held in the village.

The heavily restored church across the road from the hall probably dates

Fenny Bentley Hall

from the 14th century and contains an ornate screen which may have come from the Beresford Chantry, which was founded in 1511. But the most impressive feature is the Beresford tomb, which represents Sir Thomas, his wife Agnes, and their twenty-one children, all completely shrouded.

The Coach and Horses public house on the main road dates from the 16th century and is a former coaching inn, which must have been much is demand for teams going up or down the steep hill towards Buxton.

FINDERN (South Derbyshire)

SK3030: 3 miles (5km) SW of Derby

The legend of Findern dates back to the days of the Crusades, and concerns a small white flower which still grows in certain of the village's gardens. Sir Geoffrey de Fynderne, lord of the manor, is said to have brought back the short-stemmed, yellow-centred double narcissus when he returned from the Holy Land, and planted them on his estate. They flourished and multiplied, and although nothing now remains of the proud Fyndernes or their manor house, the flower, which has been identified as Narcissus poeticus plenus odoration or 'Poet's Daffodil', still occasionally blooms in village gardens.

Although now mainly a commuter village for Derby, Findern is one of the few South Derbyshire villages to retain its village green, which was restored and surrounded by posts and chains in 1966-67. **Somerville** (private) is a good 18th-century listed house in Findern's Main Street. It is believed that Jedediah Strutt, later to be a partner with Richard Arkwright and founder his great mill at Belper, served his apprenticeship as a wheelwright here. Another house of note, **Tower House**, stands on the hill outside the village and was formerly the village windmill. Just across the ever-busy A38 trunk road from Findern is the massive Toyota car factory, which provides much local employment.

The only thing that Sir Geoffrey Fynderne might recognise in the **parish church of All Saints** is the small, crudely carved, Norman tympanum which is now in the wall of the north aisle. Little else remains of the original medieval church after it was almost entirely rebuilt in 1863. The octagonal font dates from 1666.

FOOLOW (Derbyshire Dales)

SK1876: 6 miles (10km) N of Bakewell

It is often the source of some amusement to visitors that just to the west of Foolow is the small dry valley known as **Silly Dale**. In fact, the name of Foolow has nothing to do with the inhabitants' intelligence – it comes from the Old English and probably means 'multi-coloured hill'. This small, nucleated village on the limestone plateau between Eyam and Tideswell clusters around its village pond, or 'mere', which in turn is watched over by a crocketed medieval cross.

Foolow can claim to be one of the prettiest villages in Derbyshire: the large green is surrounded by some fine 17th- and 18th-century cottages, the most important of which are the bay-windowed, 17th-century **Manor House**, and the **Old Hall**. During that period of the village's heyday, lead mining combined with farming as the major occupation of the inhabitants, and there is still much evidence of their spoil heaps and shafts in the surrounding meadows. The village well-dressing takes place in late August.

The small **parish church** has an un-usual dedication to St Hugh, and was built in 1888. The Wesleyan Reform Chapel was built in 1836 and has a grand, Tuscan-style porch and thin, lancet-type side windows.

FOREMARK (South Derbyshire)

SK3326: 5 miles (8km) S of Derby

Foremark is not really a village, but an annexe of the nearby public school of Repton. **Foremark Hall** is the preparatory school for Repton and was built around 1760 in the fashionable Palladian style by Sir Robert Burdett, to a design by David Hiorns. With seven bays and cupolas at the corners, Foremark Hall is entered by fine, wrought-iron gates by Robert Bakewell of Derby.

The **parish church of St Saviour** is an interesting example of 17th-century Gothic Revival architecture, and the interior contains original box pews, a three-decker pulpit and an ornate chancel screen.

To the north, in the valley of the River Trent, is **Anchor Church.** This is not a church at all, but a two-roomed cave, complete with windows, which has been carved into the low sandstone cliffs by the river. The cave was traditionally used by an 'anchorite' or hermit during the Middle Ages. The burial of 'Ye fool at Anchor Church' is recorded at Repton Church in 1658, so it may have been used as a hermitage well into the 17th century. Today, the cave and its associated Black Pool in the river are the lonely haunts of heron and the occasional angler.

FROGGATT (Derbyshire Dales)

SK2476: 5 miles (8km) NE of Bakewell

The Froggatt Show, held on August Bank Holiday Saturday, is the highlight of the year in this small village which stands beneath the frowning gritstone escarpment of **Froggatt Edge**, on the well-wooded banks of the Derwent. The show has agricultural roots and was founded in the 1930s as an offshoot of the village 'Cow Club', but now its exhibits are mainly horticultural, reflecting the change in village society.

The bridge over the River Derwent dates from the 17th century and is unusual in that it has a large central arch nearer to the village and a smaller one on the other side, which probably formed part of the original bridge. This was constructed when the river was narrower, before the Derwent was dammed downstream for the mill at Calver.

The **Wesleyan Reform Chapel** is the major building of note in the village, which uses All Saints Parish Church at nearby Curbar for its established Church services.

GLOSSOP (High Peak)

SK0393: 9 miles (14km) N of Chapel-en-le-Frith

Priding itself on the description 'the gateway to the Peak', Glossop is an ancient settlement at the western end of the **Doctor's Gate** Roman road. The route was followed by the 1821 turnpike road known as the Snake Pass. This is one of the highest and most desolate roads in Derbyshire, passing between Kinder Scout and Bleaklow, and frequently receives mentions in winter weather reports when it is closed because of snowdrifts.

The original settlement at Glossop grew up around the Roman fort of **Melandra**, which is situated about a mile north-west of the present town centre, on the edge of the vast Manchester overspill council housing estate at Gamesley. Dating from about 75AD, the fort was probably constructed to guard the trans-Pennine route between Navio at Brough in the Hope Valley and Manchester. Nothing now remains except the foundations, but the site commands a fine view east towards the pass of Longdendale.

Old Glossop, on the eastern side of the modern town, still retains the air of the original old market town, and consists of some fine 17th-century gritstone cottages grouped around the **parish church of All Saints**. Only one arch in the north aisle remains of the original medieval church, which was extensively rebuilt in 1853 by the Duke of Norfolk, whose arms feature in the spandrels of the tower.

The modern town of Glossop owes almost everything to the enterprise of the Howard family, the major landowners during the first quarter of the 19th century. It was Bernard Edward Howard, the 12th Duke of Norfolk, who together with a number of other local entrepreneurs established the first cotton mills in Glossopdale. By 1831, there were no less than thirty mills in the town, and the industrial area to the west of Old Glossop became known as **Howard Town**, in recognition of the family's influence. This was a time of enormous expansion and prosperity for the town, and the dignified town hall (built in 1838) in The Square in the

The Market Hall, Glossop

centre of the town dates from this period. Two years earlier, the Duke had built the Roman Catholic church of All Saints in Church Terrace, in a severely neo-Greek style, with Tuscan pilasters and pediment. The granting of the borough charter in 1866 marked the high point of Glossop's prosperity, which lasted until the collapse of the cotton trade in the 1920s. There is still some light industry in Glossop, but the cotton mills have gone and the town has reverted to the pleasant market town it was before the cotton trade and the Howard family made it a centre of the Industrial Revolution.

GREAT HUCKLOW (Derbyshire Dales)

SK1777: 6 miles (10km) N of Bakewell

This former lead mining village under **Hucklow Edge** was once known all over the country for its outstanding amateur dramatic group known as the **Hucklow Players**. The group was the inspiration of Dr Laurence du Garde Peach, a well-known author, playwright and dramatist, who lived at nearby Housely and whose father was the local minister. The Players, all of whom were local people, performed in the Unitarian Holiday Home in the village until 1938, when they moved to a converted lead mining cupola barn which became the new playhouse. Plays were often performed in the Derbyshire dialect, which may have made them sometimes difficult to understand to audiences which came from as far away as Stratford-upon-Avon and Harrogate for performances. To aid local people, plays were often put on to coincide with the full moon because most of the audience had to walk home to the neighbouring villages after the performance. The playhouse is now used as a Scout centre for visiting groups.

Great Hucklow's primary school

was built in 1873 on a lead mine hillock – another reminder of the days when the village was a centre of the lead mining industry. At Camphill Farm, high on Hucklow Edge above the village, the Derbyshire and Lancashire Gliding Club has its lofty headquarters, and the sight of the graceful gliders riding the thermals often fills the skies above the village. The club, founded in 1935, was one of the earliest in the country, and occupies one of the most spectacular launching sites at over 1360ft (415m) above the sea. Also on Hucklow Edge is **The Barrel Inn**, in the parish of Bretton, which is one of the highest and oldest pubs in Derbyshire, dating from 1637. It enjoys spectacular views across the White Peak limestone plateau.

GREAT LONGSTONE (Derbyshire Dales)

SK1971: 2 miles (3km) N of Bakewell

Great Longstone is a typical one-street White Peak village. The street, with some good 18th-century cottages, winds up to a linear, roadside green. Another lead mining centre, Longstone's wealth was based on the ore won by generations of miners from nearby **Longstone Edge**, which until recently was still being quarried for fluorspar – a mineral the lead miners rejected as waste. At the top of the village street, behind a high brick wall, is the handsome Georgian manor house of **Longstone Hall**, built in 1747 (private). The **parish church of St Giles** and the Crispin Inn, opposite the hall, are reminders of another of Longstone's traditional trades, that of boot and shoemaking. The church is medieval, dating from the 13th century, but restored in 1873. Inside are memorials to the Wright and Eyre families. It also serves the neighbouring villages of Hassop, Rowland, Wardlow and Little Longstone.

GRINDLEFORD (Derbyshire Dales)

SK2477: 6 miles (10km) N of Bakewell

The name of this charming little Derwent-side village is probably connected to the grindstones which were made in local quarries for many years from the abrasive gritstone of the nearby 'edges'. It may mean the ford near to where the grindstones were made, but no one can be sure. Grindleford occupies a lovely position between Eyam Moor and Froggatt Edge, and includes in its parish the beautiful **Padley Gorge** (National Trust), famous for its sessile oakwoods and pied flycatcher summer migrants. Also in the hamlet of Upper Padley is the simple little barn-like structure of **Padley Chapel**, which was formerly the gatehouse of Padley Hall, the medieval manor house of the Eyre and Fitzherbert families. It was the scene in 1588 of one of the worst of the Roman Catholic persecutions during Elizabeth I's reign. Two Catholic priests, Nicholas Garlick and Robert Ludlam, were being hidden here by Sir Thomas Fitzherbert of Norbury (see NORBURY), but they were discovered, arrested and taken to Derby to be hanged, drawn and quartered for their beliefs. An annual 'Padley Pilgrimage' is held every July to mark this horrific deed, and the event is centred on the chapel, which was bought by the Roman Catholic Diocese of Nottingham in 1933. It is still an evocative spot. Nearby is the mouth of the **Totley Railway Tunnel,** which passes under the moors to Sheffield. Over three miles in length, it was one of the longest in Britain when it was opened in 1893.

Grindleford village is strung out for about two miles along the river and down to the fine three-arched bridge which spans the mighty Derwent. The village has a lively social life, which is reflected in the construction of the Bishop Pavilion near the cricket field and the bridge. It was named after its major benefactor, local businessman Eric Bishop, and is in almost constant use.

HADFIELD (High Peak)

SK0296: 1 mile (2km) NW of Glossop

Hadfield is a small village near Glossop, standing at the western entrance to Longdendale, one of the major trans-Pennine routes through history. It is now the terminus of the **Longdendale Trail,** part of the Trans-Pennine Trail, a west-east walking, riding and cycling 'leisure route' which follows the line of the former Great Central Line Woodhead Railway. The railway was constructed in 1847 at great loss of life to the navvies. Some of their graves can still be seen at the isolated **Woodhead Chapel,** 5 miles (8km) west of the village above the Woodhead Reservoir in Longdendale. When the string of five reservoirs in Longdendale – Bottoms, Valehouse, Rhodeswood, Torside and Woodhead – were completed in 1877,

they constituted the largest man-made stretch of water in the world.

The oldest building in Hadfield village, which is a pleasing mixture of old and new, is the Stuart **Old Hall** in The Square, which bears a date stone of 1646 over the door. A number of textile mills were built in Hadfield during the Industrial Revolution, but all are now closed. The village became part of the estate of the Dukes of Norfolk, and the Victorian Roman Catholic **church of St Charles** was built by Baron Howard of Glossop in 1868. Various members of the Howard family are buried in the church.

HARTINGTON (Derbyshire Dales)

SK1360: 9 miles (14km) SE of Buxton

Hartington, at the northern end of Dovedale, still wears the air of a prosperous market town, although it is nearly 800 years since its market charter was first granted and many years since a market was last held in its spacious square. The classical, three-arched façade of the **Town Hall,** built in 1836, adds to this urban impression. The Square is ringed by elegant 18th- and 19th-century stone cottages.

The **Charles Cotton Hotel** is a reminder of one of Hartington's most famous sons, co-author with Izaak Walton of *The Compleat Angler,* who lived at Beresford Hall (of which only an ornate fishing lodge remains) in nearby Beresford Dale. Just west of The Square is the **Hartington Cheese Factory,** one of a handful in the country licensed to produce Stilton cheese. There is a shop and visitor centre which explains the long process involved in producing the famous blue-veined 'King of English cheeses'.

Another famous visitor to Hartington was Prince Charles Edward Stuart (Bonnie Prince Charlie) on his ill-fated march on London in 1645. He is alleged to have stayed at the lovely Tudor mansion of **Hartington Hall**, south-east of the village centre, which is now surely one of the most palatial youth hostels in the country. Hartington Hall was built by Robert Bateman in 1611, and is a typical Derbyshire three-gabled, stone-mullioned manor house.

The hilltop **parish church of St Giles** is one of the most interesting in the county, with a two-storey porch, transepts and aisles dating mainly from the 13th and 14th centuries. The massive and dignified battlemented Perpendicular west tower stands watch over the village below. It stands at the centre of one of the biggest parishes in the country, divided into four quarters – Town, Upper, Nether and Middle.

HARTSHORNE (South Derbyshire)

SK3221: 1 mile (2km) NE of Swadlincote

The name is thought to have been derived from Horn Hill, south-east of the village, and its supposed resemblance to a hart's horn. Housing from nearby Swadlincote and Woodville is gradually creeping near to this previously isolated spot, but it retains a village character, especially around the church and half-timbered **Manor House**.

The **parish church of St Peter** has a 15th-century tower, but was heavily restored in 1835, with cast-iron tracery in the lancet windows. An important monument inside is that to Sir Humphrey Dethick, who died in 1599, his wife and six children, standing around the tomb-chest.

HASSOP (Derbyshire Dales)

SK2272: 2 miles (3km) N of Bakewell

Standing like a little Grecian temple stranded in the heart of the Peak District, the Roman Catholic **church of All Saints** always comes as something of a surprise. The reason for the presence of this Classical Revival building, with its Etruscan temple front and Tuscan pilasters at the rear, lies just across the road at **Hassop Hall**, an elegant early 17th-century house which was the family seat of the staunchly Catholic Eyre family. The church was built in 1816 and contains under its coved and coffered ceiling a wonderful painting of the Crucifixion by Lodovico Carracci, and a fine monument to its founder, Thomas Eyre, who died in 1833.

Hassop Hall, now a hotel and restaurant, is a fine, three-storeyed country house standing within its own landscaped park. Inside there are marble chimney pieces by White Watson of nearby Ashford-in-the-Water, and some excellent early 19th-century plasterwork. Just below the hall, on the road to Bakewell, stands **The Dower House**, an imposing, late 17th-century, three-gabled house which used to be the village post office, but which has now been converted into luxury flats. The Eyre Arms is a popular hostelry on the road to Calver and is clad with a vivid scarlet Virginia creeper in the late summer and autumn.

HATHERSAGE
(Derbyshire Dales)

SK2381: 8 miles (13km) N of Bakewell

Hathersage stands on the A625 at the eastern entrance to the wide Hope Valley. It takes its name from the Old English for 'Haefer's ridge' – a probable reference to the moorland slopes of **Stanage Edge** which frown down on this bustling little village. Once the centre of a thriving needle and pin making industry, Hathersage has returned to its rural peace, only interrupted by the constant tourist traffic heading for Castleton from Sheffield. The village was also an important centre for mill and grindstone making, and the unfinished and abandoned remains of these massive stones are still to be found scattered at the foot of the Edges. There are many

connections with Charlotte Brontë in and around the village. She often came to Hathersage to stay with her friend Ellen Nussey at the Vicarage, and is thought to have based the town 'Morton' in *Jane Eyre* on Hathersage. **North Lees Hall** (private), a fine, embattled Tudor tower house a mile and a half north-east of the village, beneath Stanage Edge, is thought to have been Charlotte's model for Thornfield Hall, Mr Rochester's home in the same book. It is now used by the Derbyshire College of Agriculture as a model farm, and the house is let as a holiday home by the Vivat Trust. In fact, North Lees Hall is one of seven Eyre halls around Hathersage, all thought to have been built by Robert Eyre for his sons and all within sight of one another.

The Eyre family features strongly in the **parish church of St Michael**, which stands on its hilltop site, aloof from the main village. It has a battlemented, 15th-century Perpendicular tower with a graceful spire, but dates mainly from the 14th century. The east window, with its stained glass by Thomas Kempe, was taken from the church at Derwent when it was submerged under the rising waters of the Ladybower Reservoir, further up the valley.

The brasses to the Eyre family in Hathersage church are among the finest in the county. Deserving special mention is that of Robert Eyre, who died in 1459, complete in his plate armour, and

Hathersage Parish Church

that of the builder of the hall, Robert Eyre, of around 1500.

Outside the south door of the church, visitors are shown what is reputed to be the **grave of Little John,** Robin Hood's loyal henchman, who is alleged to have been born in Hathersage. The 'grave' has been adopted by the Ancient Order of Foresters, who come to pay annual tribute. Sadly, there is no historical evidence that Little John – nor indeed Robin Hood – ever existed, although believers will also point to Robin Hood's Cave on nearby Stanage Edge. But this airy gritstone balcony is more often the haunt of bivouacking rock-climbers today, than it ever was a refuge for the fictional medieval outlaw.

HATTON (South Derbyshire)

SK2130: 9 miles (14km) SW of Derby

Hatton is in the valley of the Lower Dove, opposite castle-crowned Tutbury, across the border in Staffordshire, and its past is closely linked with that town. They are linked by the five-arched **Hatton Bridge,** which dates from the 19th century, but is a replacement for a much older structure which Mary Queen of Scots might have known when she was imprisoned at Tutbury. Today, Hatton is bisected by the busy A50 Burton-Stoke trunk road, and the main source of local employment is the Nestlé Factory, built in 1901. Victorian **All Saints Parish Church** was built by a Mr Gould of Tutbury in 1886, and the Methodist church in 1912.

HAYFIELD (High Peak)

SK0386: 5 miles (8km) S of Glossop

Hayfield stands at the crossroads of a number of formerly important moorland routes. It was once a stopping place for coaches between Glossop and Buxton, and is also on one of the main packhorse routes between Cheshire and Yorkshire, reflected in the name of the **Pack Horse Inn,** built in 1577 on the Kinder Road.

Best known today by walkers as the starting point for the popular western ascent of Derbyshire's highest point of Kinder Scout (2088ft/636m), the neat little gritstone township at the junction of the Rivers Sett and Kinder has played an historic part in rambling folklore. It was from here, **Bowden Bridge Quarry** west of the village centre to be precise, on April 24 1932 that the famous Kinder Scout Mass Trespass set out to exercise the ramblers' right to roam on the then forbidden moorland. Five ramblers were later arrested and imprisoned for their part in the demonstration. A small commemorative plaque was erected in the quarry to mark the 50th anniversary. Ironically, the quarry now serves as a car park for walkers.

Hayfield was formerly a centre of industry, with wool, cotton, papermaking and textile printing mills using the fast flowing waters of the Sett and Kinder. All these industries are long gone today, but the fine Georgian **parish church of St Matthew** gives a hint of the former prosperity of this little Pennine town. Rebuilt in 1818 in the style popular at the time, the chancel was added in 1894. Inside, the gallery on three sides is supported by thin cast-iron columns and there are box pews. The churchyard was the scene of two 'resurrections' within three years of each other during the 18th century.

Hayfield, with Parish Church

In 1745, several witnesses attested to seeing hundreds of bodies rise out of their graves and ascend into heaven. Three years later, there was a disastrous flood, which ripped through the churchyard and disinterred many bodies, which were then swept away downstream. Flooding has always been a problem in Hayfield, and the present Town Bridge, built in 1837, is the third on the site, replacing two which had been swept away in the past.

The **Royal Hotel** in the village centre has twice been a parsonage, and John Wesley stayed there in 1755. The small square off Market Street is known as Dungeon Brow because the village lock-up was situated in a corner. Three-gabled **Fox Hall** was built in 1525, and **Park Hall**, one mile north of the village, is a handsome seven-bay, two-storeyed house with an Ionic colonnaded entrance. It was built in 1811.

Hayfield was the venue for two annual cattle and sheep fairs in the past, but all that remains now is the **Hayfield Sheepdog Trials and Country Fair**, held every September at Spray House Farm. Hayfield also holds a popular Jazz Festival. The village is now split into two by the A624 Buxton-Glossop road, and the western side is now largely made up of suburban houses for people working in nearby Manchester.

One of Hayfield's most famous sons was the actor **Arthur Lowe**, Captain Mainwaring in television's 'Dad's Army'. He was a member of the village cricket team, and regularly brought members of the cast to play the village team on the delightfully situated village cricket ground on the Kinder Road.

HAZELWOOD (Amber Valley)

SK3245: 7 miles (11km) N of Derby

Hazelwood lies high on the ridge between the Rivers Derwent and Ecclesbourne, and commands fine views towards Crich Stand. There is evidence that the Romans settled here: archaeologists have found Roman kilns, a lead smelting hearth and the possible remains of a villa in **Jenny Tang Wood**. Today, Hazelwood is a pleasant residential village for Derby, but it has had some famous occupants. These include Sir John Gay Newton, the engineer responsible for the soaring roof of St Pancras Station in London, who lived at Chevin House, at the foot of the hill east of the village; and Mrs E.M. Hull, who lived at The Knowle and was the author of *The Sheik* and *Sons of the Sheik*, both of which were made into films starring Rudolph Valentino.

The **parish church of St John,** with its little bellcote, stands at the crossroads in the centre of the village. It was originally built in 1846, but severely damaged by a fire in 1902 and rebuilt in the same year.

HEAGE (Amber Valley)

SK3650: 2 miles (3km) W of Ripley

The strange-sounding name of Heage comes from the Old English and means 'high edge or ridge' – a perfect description of the situation of this village set on rising ground above the River Derwent east of Ambergate. Formerly High Heage and Low or Nether Heage, the village is still split into two main parts, neither of which has a real centre. The most famous feature is **Heage Windmill** – a real rarity in Derbyshire, and a handsome tower mill which has been tastefully restored by Derbyshire County Council. The gritstone tower, topped by its silver ogee cap and, unusually, six wooden sails was built by Edmund Lee in 1745. There is a small vaned wheel at the back of the cap, set at right angles to the sails, which is designed to turn the sails into the wind.

Heage's other interesting monuments to industrial archaeology are the twin pyramidical, flat-topped stone blast furnaces built in 1810 and 1818 into the side of a grassy hill to the south-east of the village. These are all that remains of the Morley Park Ironworks, built towards the end of the 18th century by Francis Hurt of Alderwasley Hall, across the valley.

Earlier than these strange monuments to the Industrial Age is **Heage Hall** at Nether Heage, which dates back to the 15th century and is now a farm. The **parish church of St Luke** originally dated from the Middle Ages, but it was mostly destroyed in a storm in 1545 and rebuilt in 1616. It was greatly enlarged in 1836, with the later addition of a strange, polygonal belltower – so it now represents an odd mixture of styles and ages.

HEANOR (Amber Valley)

SK4346: 5 miles (8km) E of Belper

Heanor is a grim industrial town close to the Nottinghamshire border. It was founded on the riches won from coal and iron working, all of which is now gone. It stands on a hilltop above the valley of the River Erewash, and its Market Square is a reminder of the days when it was nothing more than a country market town. The tall, 15th-century Perpendicular tower of the **parish church of St Lawrence** is a further reminder of Heanor's medieval past, but most of the rest of the church dates from an extensive 1868 rebuilding. Inside, there is an interesting monument to Samuel Watson, who died in 1715 and who was the wood-carver whose exquisite work at Chatsworth is often compared with that of Grinling Gibbons.

The Georgian red-brick, three-bayed Wesleyan Chapel dates from 1839. All Saints at Marlpool, south of the town centre, is a late Victorian church which was tastefully rebuilt after a fire. St Andrew's Parish Church at nearby Langley Mill is an Arts and Crafts Gothic church of great interest. It was built in 1912.

HEATH (North East Derbyshire)

SK4466: 5 miles (8km) SE of Chesterfield

Overshadowed by the roaring traffic of Junction 29 of the M1, Heath is another of those north-east Derbyshire villages which was ravaged by the coal industry, both above and below ground. The adjacent mining village of **Holmewood**, to the west, was built to house the workers of the now-defunct Hardwick Colliery, and effectively tripled the population of the village overnight. The 1960s saw the scourge of opencast mining round the village, which destroyed many of the old field patterns, trees and ponds of countryside which had not changed much since it was first recorded in the Domesday Book as 'Lunt' or 'Lound', meaning 'a grove' or 'small wood'.

The **parish church of All Saints**, with its spire, dates from 1853 and took the place of an earlier building, a quarter of a mile away down the hill. All that is left of the original building are some ancient, perhaps 12th-century, carved stone coffin slabs in the porch, one featuring a crucifix.

HIGHAM (North East Derbyshire)

SK3959: 8 miles (13km) S of Chesterfield

Higham was granted a charter to hold a weekly market as long ago as 1243, and until the outbreak of the Second World War, it still held an annual cattle fair on the first Wednesday of the New Year. The venerable **market cross**, with its flight of seven steps, is a reminder of those days when this pleasant little village off the A61 Derby-Chesterfield road was still a basically agricultural community. The cross, originally medieval, was repaired in 1755 at a cost of three shillings and sixpence (17.5p). But although Higham is now mainly residential in character, it has retained many of its older buildings, and the village centre is now designated as a conservation area.

HOGNASTON (Derbyshire Dales)

SK2350: 4 miles (6km) NE of Ashbourne

The village of Hognaston is overshadowed by the massive embankment of the Carsington Reservoir, opened in 1992 (see CARSINGTON). But although the building of the reservoir resulted in much loss of land to the village, the new roads associated with

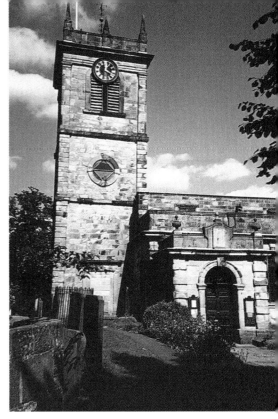

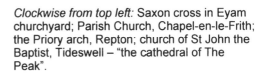

Clockwise from top left: Saxon cross in Eyam churchyard; Parish Church, Chapel-en-le-Frith; the Priory arch, Repton; church of St John the Baptist, Tideswell – "the cathedral of The Peak".

From top: the only cottage left from the original village of Edensor, now in Chatsworth Park; Chatsworth House, from the Park; an abandoned millstone on Curbar Edge, looking down on Calver,

From top: Grindslow Knoll (left) and Kinder Scout from Mam Tor, with Edale village (centre); the market place and monument, Melbourne; Parish Church, Hope, with Lose Hill in the background

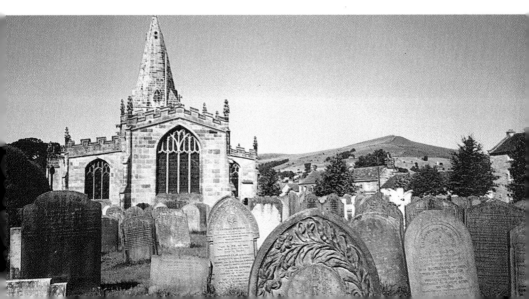

Above: Nag's Head Inn, Edale

Right: Eyam Parish Church

Below: North Lees Hall, Hathersage

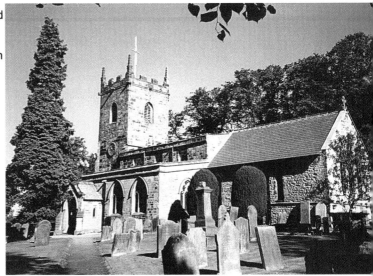

it effectively bypassed the village, returning it to its rural peace. Built on the spring line on a south-facing slope, Hognaston is an ancient settlement, and has a number of fine, 17th-century, stone-built cottages opposite the church. The **parish church of St Bartholomew** is one of the oldest and most interesting parish churches in Derbyshire. Built on a raised site in the centre of the village, the church is famous for its amazing Norman doorway, featuring a tympanum which shows what appears to be a bishop with his crook, a lamb with crosses, two fishes and a boar with several other wild beasts. The west tower of the church, four-square and unbuttressed, dates from the 13th century, with a Perpendicular top and Victorian pinnacles. Inside, the chancel arch dates from the 14th century and the tub-shaped font is Norman, with sunken arches.

HOLBROOK (Amber Valley)

SK3645: 2 miles (3km) S of Belper

On the high ground between the busy A6 and A38 trunk roads, Holbrook commands fine views. It takes its name from the Old English for 'the brook in the hollow' – the brook being Bottle Brook – and a Romano-British pottery kiln has been excavated in the grounds of **Holbrook Hall**. The hall was a Classically-inspired stone house built in 1681, and is two storeys high with five bays and a pedimented doorway. It was largely rebuilt in 1841, and further enlarged with art nouveau embellishments in the early 20th century.

The **parish church of St Michael** grew from what was originally the Georgian chapel of the hall, and stands above it. It was largely rebuilt in 1841, when it was much altered and enlarged. There are some fine Spanish chestnut trees in the churchyard.

HOLLOWAY (Amber Valley)

SK3256: 3 miles (5km) SE of Matlock

Forever associated with its most famous daughter, Holloway was the home of the Crimean war nursing heroine **Florence Nightingale**, who lived at **Leahurst**. This 17th-century gabled house with low mullioned windows was greatly enlarged by her father in 1825. Although Florence was born in the city of that name in Italy, she spent most of her childhood here, and returned almost anonymously to Holloway after she came back from the Crimea in 1856.

The Nightingale family was actively involved in village life, and provided the site for the Florence Nightingale Memorial Hall, built in 1932, and a social centre for the hillside village. **Lea Wood** is another fine Victorian house nearby, while **Lea Hall**, a mile away to the north, is a five-bayed early Georgian house with Roman Doric pilasters and pedimented door. **Christ Church**, Holloway, has been described as the finest of P.H. Currey's churches in Derbyshire. It was built by the Smedley family of nearby Lea Bridge in 1903, and has a large crossing tower and mock-Perpendicular details.

Close by the village are the popular **Lea Rhododendron Gardens**, a blaze of colour and thronged with admiring visitors in early summer.

HOLMESFIELD (North East Derbyshire)

SK3277: 5 miles (8km) NW of Chesterfield

Holmesfield lies on the high road which crosses Totley Moor on the edge of Sheffield, where it rears up to meet the Peak District hills. It is undoubtedly part of Sheffield's famous 'Golden Frame' – the often-used description of the lovely countryside which surrounds the industrial city. Holmesfield is a scattered village with no real centre and consists of a number of small, former farming hamlets above the Cordwell Valley, overlooking the tower blocks of Sheffield to the north. The major settlements are at **Millthorpe**, **Cowley Bar** and **Norwoods**.

One of Holmesfield's most famous sons was Robert Murray Gilchrist, a Sheffield man who became one of Derbyshire's best-known novelists. He lived at the Elizabethan farmhouse of Cartledge Hall (private), which has original panelling and plasterwork inside. Another famous resident of Norwood was another Sheffield-born man, G.H.B. ('Bert') Ward, the so-called 'King of the Clarion Ramblers', who was secretary and leading light of this early and influential rambling club from its inception in 1900. Among Holmesfield's important buildings are **Holmesfield Hall**, dated 1613, but with an 18th-century frontage, and **Woodthorpe Hall**, a large, L-shaped, 17th-century, gabled manor house, dated 1636, and a home of the Fanshawe family.

If there is a natural centre to the village, it is around the **parish church of St Swithin**, which was built in 1826 with a Victorian-Gothic pinnacled tower. The nave has Georgian-style windows, and the chancel was added in 1895 and enlarged again in 1963, with modern stained glass.

HOLYMOORSIDE (North East Derbyshire)

SK3369: 3 miles (5km) W of Chesterfield

Now not much more than a commuter village for nearby Chesterfield and Sheffield, Holymoorside was once a thriving industrial centre, with Manlove's three cotton thread mills dominating the village. Nothing remains now except **The Dam**, the millpond for the mills, which is now a popular spot for recreation and especially for local anglers. The 'Holy' of Holymoorside comes from the fact that in medieval times monks from Beauchief Abbey near Sheffield were sent to **Harewood Grange**, on the western side of the village, if they had transgressed the strict rules of the abbey. Harewood Grange, now a farm, was a monastic 'house of correction'. The 'moorside' part of the village name is obvious because it is situated on the edge of heather-clad Beeley Moor, and what is now the Peak District National Park. Another older building of note in the village is **Hipper Hall**, a 16th-century farmhouse with an ancient tithe barn, which takes its name from the local river. There are three Victorian churches in Holymoorside: the **parish church of St Peter's**; the United Reformed Church and the Methodist Chapel. Most of the social life of the village revolves around the village school built by the Manloves in 1874, and the large modern Village Hall by the Recreation Ground.

HOPE (High Peak)

SK1783: 1 mile (2km) E of Castleton

The former importance of the village of Hope can be judged by the fact that it gave its name to the entire Hope Valley, which stretches from Castleton, now a more important village, to Hathersage. At the time that the Domesday Book was written, Hope boasted both a priest and a church, a rare distinction for Derbyshire, thirty villagers, four smallholders and a mill. Hope was an important centre of the Royal Forest of the Peak, a hunting preserve of medieval kings and princes, which was administered from nearby Castleton. Two 13th-century cross slabs in the church are thought to carry the symbols of Royal Forest officials, or 'woodruffes'. Also in the churchyard of the **parish church of St Peter**, is a fine, although headless, Saxon cross, with interlacing knotwork thought to date from the 9th century. The church itself dates mainly from the 14th century, and has a fine, though stumpy, broach spire. The chancel, with fine stained glass by Kempe, was rebuilt in 1882, but it incorporates a piscina and sedilia of the early 14th century. The font is all that remains from the original Norman church mentioned in the Domesday Book.

Earlier still are the remains of the earthworks of the Roman fort of Navio at nearby **Brough**, a mile away to the east. This was a small, rectangular fort built in the first century AD, probably to control the Romans' lead mining interests in the area.

The **Old Hall Hotel** in the village centre was originally the Old Hall of the Balguy family, while the Woodruffe Arms commemorates those local fami-

Saxon cross, Hope church

lies remembered in the church who served the Royal Forest. **Aston Hall** is an Elizabethan manor house, dated 1578, with an unusual, three-light, pedimented window incorporating a worn, carved figure. It is in the neighbouring hamlet, overlooking the village on the slopes of Win Hill.

Farming is still the most important industry in Hope, as it has been for a thousand years or more. There is a preserved **pinfold**, where stray animals were penned, on the Pin Dale road behind the church, and the twice-weekly Hope Market brings in cattle and sheep for sale from the surrounding farms. Even more come to the **Hope Agricultural Show,** which is held annually on

August Bank Holiday Monday. Hope retains its importance in the life of the valley with the large, modern Hope Valley College comprehensive school, built in 1958 on the Castleton Road.

HOPTON (Derbyshire Dales)

SK2553: 2 miles (3km) W of Wirksworth

Hopton is the ancestral home of the famous Derbyshire family of the Gells, who gave us the Via Gellia leading up from Cromford to Grangemill and, by association, Viyella hosiery (see BONSALL), and the Anthony Gell School at Wirksworth.

Hopton Hall, a gabled, Elizabethan house, altered in the Georgian style in the late 18th century, has been the Gell's family seat since the early 14th century. It was the home of such notables as Sir John Gell, a distinguished Parliamentary general during the Civil War, and Sir William Gell, a classical scholar and friend of Walter Scott, Lord Byron, and Thomas Moore, who was born here in 1777. Sir Phillip Gell built the range of almshouses for two men and two women from the village in 1722, and there are a number of interesting stone-built cottages in the village. But Hopton today, like nearby Carsington, is overshadowed by the huge Carsington Reservoir, on its southern border.

HORSLEY (Amber Valley)

SK3744: 5 miles (8km) N of Derby

Approached from the east, the fine broach spire of the **parish church of St Clement and St James** dominates the village from its hilltop site. The embat-tled Perpendicular exterior dates mainly from the mid-15th century, although the arches in the nave are 14th century.

Horsley retains its village atmosphere, complete with traditional village green and spreading chestnut tree, despite the proximity of Derby and the industrial Erewash valley. The Wesleyan Methodist Chapel is a small but attractive stone-built building facing the village green. It was opened in 1845. The church of England School was opened in 1828 and enlarged in 1874.

Among the village's most prized features are its rare **stone pillar box** in French Lane, and the **three fountains**, named Blanch, Sophie and Rosamund after the daughters of the Reverend Sitwell, who bequeathed them to the village in 1864. Horsley's former importance is evidenced by the fact that it once had a castle known as Horeston at nearby Coxbench. It was owned by Montforts, Shirleys, and the Dukes of Lancaster and Norfolk at various times. Nothing now remains of this powerful medieval stronghold.

HULLAND (Derbyshire Dales)

SK2447: 4 miles (6km) E of Ashbourne

Split by the A517 Ashbourne-Belper road, Hulland (more correctly Hulland Ward) is the centre of a number of smaller hamlets such as Hulland, Hulland Moss, Millington Green and Biggin. It was once the Ward or Wood Gate of the medieval Royal Forest of Duffield, and many of these hamlets date back to that period. The village is dominated by the **parish church of**

Christ Church, which stands isolated and on high ground west of the main village centre. It was built in 1851 as a plain, rectangular, aisleless building with lancet windows and an embattled west tower, from which the views are said to extend to The Wrekin in Shropshire, over forty miles away. Before 1853, Hulland was an outlying chapelry of St Oswald's Church in Ashbourne. The village school was built next to the church in 1863.

IDRIDGEHAY (Amber Valley)

SK2849: 3 miles (5km) S of Wirksworth

In the pretty valley of the Ecclesbourne, south of Wirksworth, Idridgehay, includes the hamlets of Ireton Wood and Alton. Its unusual name comes from the Old English and means 'Eadric's forest enclosure'. In ancient times it was part of the Royal Forest of Duffield, or Duffield Frith, as was neighbouring Hulland. Evidence of the antiquity of this charming village is the thatched, timber-framed house built by George Mellor in 1621 and known as **South Sitch**. The **Black Swan** public house, standing opposite in the main street, is another old building and claims to have been mentioned in George Eliot's *Adam Bede*. The Victorian **parish church of St James** has an elegant spire and was built in 1855 with funds provided by Robert Cresswell, a later occupant of South Sitch, and James Milton of **Alton Manor**. The latter is a gabled and pinnacled tower house by Sir Gilbert Scott and stands in its parkland a mile to the north. One of the biggest events in Idridgehay's recent history was the coming of the Midland Railway in 1867. The line, with its double-width bridges and large cutting east of the village, is now nothing more than a disused branch line, abandoned when the main line eventually followed the Derwent Valley through Belper to the east.

Idridgehay was unlucky enough to receive a direct hit from a land mine dropped by the Luftwaffe in 1941. It destroyed the parsonage and another house at the eastern end of the village, and damaged the village post office and shop.

ILKESTON (Erewash)

SK4642: 7 miles (11km) NE of Derby

Nikolaus Pevsner was particularly damning of Ilkeston in his *Buildings of England: Derbyshire* volume. 'A town singularly devoid of visual attractions,' was his opinion. But even he had to devote, grudgingly one suspects, a whole page to the 'stately' **parish church of St Mark**, which dominates this hilltop town above the valley of the Erewash. The church has an interesting history. It was founded in the early years of the 13th century and the north arcade was added in the 14th. The window tracery of the east window, although heavily restored in 1855, retains its original majesty. The remarkable and rare early 14th-century stone chancel screen is one of the finest in Derbyshire. The west tower has had a chequered history since it was first constructed as part of the original church. It was remodelled in 1723, Gothicised in 1854, and then taken down and rebuilt further to the west in the major enlargement of the church in 1907-9. One of the great treasures of St Mark's is the well-preserved effigy of a cross-legged knight, who may have been Sir William de Cantelope, who died in 1309.

The **town hall,** opposite the parish church in Ilkeston's Market Place, is described as 'a modest Victorian baroque building in brick of 1868'. There are two other town churches in Ilkeston, both built by the prolific P.H. Currey. The turreted St John the Evangelist, on the Nottingham road was built in 1894, and St Bartholomew in Hallam Fields, with a saddleback tower, a year later. The stylish, modern Roman Catholic church of St Thomas was built in 1931 and is dedicated to another member of the Cantelope family.

IRONVILLE (Amber Valley)

SK4351: 2 miles (3km) E of Ripley

As the name suggests, Ironville is a 'model' village constructed by the Butterley Company, owners of the nearby Butterley Iron Works, for its employees between 1834 and 1860. It is the best example of its kind in Derbyshire, with long rows of plain brick cottages and various other amenities. These include the grand **parish church,** built in 1852; two schools built in 1850; and a recreation ground featuring the Jessop Memorial to William Jessop, the founder of the ironworks. He is also remembered by his grateful employees in a memorial window in the church. Until recently, members of the teetotal Band of Hope met at the memorial every Whit Monday.

KEDLESTON (Amber Valley)

SK2941: 5 miles (8km) NE of Derby

Kedleston Hall (National Trust) was conceived as a neo-Classical temple of the arts in the mid-18th century, and as such is the most recent and surely one of the most palatial stately homes of Derbyshire. Kedleston has been the home of the Curzon family for eight centuries, but when Sir Nathaniel Curzon, 5th baronet and 1st Lord Scarsdale, decided to replace the late 17th-century Kedleston Hall with the present building in 1758, he swept away the old village of Kedleston entirely for his landscaped parklands. All that remains is the lovely old **parish church of All Saints**, hiding behind the colonnades of the North West Pavilion of the big house. The south door of the church is Norman, with a zigzag arch and defaced tympanum, but most of the rest of the building dates from the 13th century and is filled with a remarkable sequence of memorials to the Curzon family. These begin with Sir Richard de Curzon, who died in 1275, and end with the magnificent white marble tomb in the north aisle of Lord Curzon, Viceroy of India, who died in 1925, and his wife.

Kedleston Hall is without doubt the most splendid Georgian country house in Derbyshire. The design was started by Matthew Brettingham, who was replaced by James Paine in 1761. It was Paine who was responsible for the grand Palladian porticoed north front of the house. Then the great Robert Adam was called in and it was he who designed the magnificent domed south front and the whole of the sumptuous interiors The Marble Hall, with its fluted Corinthian columns, must be one of the most magnificent entrance rooms in England. The rest of the rooms, including the Dining Room, the

Library, the State Bedroom, the Drawing Room and the Music Room, are monuments to Adam's decorative genius. The house tour includes an exhibition of architectural drawings and a special Museum of India, which features the stunning Peacock Dress worn by Lady Curzon for the Delhi Durbar in 1903, at the height of the Imperialism of the British Raj.

The grounds of the hall include Adam's elegant bridge across the lake, with a boathouse to the west and a small bathhouse a half-mile to the east.

KILLAMARSH (Bolsover)

SK4680: 7 miles (11km) N of Bolsover

Killamarsh – the name celebrates the marsh of an otherwise unknown Saxon called Cynewald – is a large industrial village close to Sheffield, in the extreme north-eastern corner of Derbyshire. The coal and steel industries where most villagers once worked have now gone, and it has reverted to the agriculture which Cynewald might have recognised. In the 1830s, Killamarsh was a well-known centre for cockfighting, and earlier still, for bull, bear and badger-baiting. An unfortunate reminder of those barbaric times is the name of the newest public house in the village – the Bull and Badger. The **parish church of St Giles** is tucked away on a side street, and dates from Norman times, as the zigzag work on the south doorway testifies. The pinnacled tower dates from the 15th century as does the charming stained glass window in the south chancel showing a crowned Madonna and child. On the outside wall of the church is a stone tablet which records the fact that John Wright, a pauper, died in 1797 at the ripe old age of 103. The Methodist church also has a fine stained glass window, which appropriatcly dcpicts a miner at work. The Congregational church, on the sloping High Street, is known locally as 'the church on the hill', while the Ebenezer Gospel Hall has the nickname of 'the church in the field'.

Just to the north of Killamarsh is the popular **Rother Valley Country Park** with its acres of open water and woodlands, created from the wasteland of former opencast coal mine workings. A more recent addition has been a dry ski slope.

KING STERNDALE (High Peak)

SK0972: 2 miles (3km) east of Buxton

This charming little limestone hamlet is in the hills high above Ashwood Dale in the valley of the Wye just outside Buxton. The road to the village ends beyond the village green, which has the battered remains of the village cross. The intimate little **parish church** was designed by Bonomi in the Gothic style and built in 1847. It has a bellcot, lancet windows and dormer lights in the roof. There is a commemorative brass to Miss Ellen Hawkins from nearby Cowdale, who founded the church, and there are other memorials to the Pickford family, including the judge, William Pickford, who became Lord Sterndale, Master of the Rolls, and died in 1923. The pretty village was threatened by the expansion of the **Topley Pike Quarry**, below the village in the valley of the Wye, until the recent news that it was to close. The great faces of the enormous quarry had almost reached the village street, but are hidden from view behind rows of beeches.

KIRK IRETON
(Derbyshire Dales)

SK2650: 4 miles (6km) S of Wirksworth

Kirk Ireton, a small limestone village in the hills south of Wirksworth, has an interesting name. It is thought to mean 'the church on the farm of the Irishman'. 'Kirk' comes from the Norse for 'church', while 'Ire-tun' probably refers to the farm of a Scandinavian who had been to Ireland, or an Irishman who accompanied the Vikings to this part of England. One of the oldest buildings in the village is the **Barley Mow** public house, a tall, gabled building dating from the 17th century. But, as usual, it is the **parish church of the Holy Trinity** which tells us most about the village's history. It is approached through the 18th-century gateway that formerly belonged to the manor house. The pinnacled, embattled tower dates from the 14th-century Perpendicular period, as does the chancel arch. There is a very attractive doorway from the chancel to the vestry with ornate mouldings around slender pillars. The south arcade, with its circular columns with moulded capitals, dates from the late Norman period. An interesting old custom is still maintained in the church – the 'roping' for weddings. Village children put a rope across the road, and the bride and groom cannot leave the church until the bridegroom pays a toll in silver.

A short distance away to the southwest is the tiny hamlet of **Blackwall**, home of the Blackwall family since the 15th century. **Blackwall Hall** is an early 19th-century, Tudor-style manor house standing in its own grounds.

KIRK LANGLEY
(Amber Valley)

SK2838: 4 miles (6km) NW of Derby

Kirk Langley is bisected by the A52 Derby-Ashbourne road and actually consists of two villages: Kirk Langley with its **parish church of St Michael**, and Meynell Langley, centred on the Victorian brick mansion of **Langley Park**, site of the home of the Meynell family for 800 years. The village pub is also known as the Meynell Arms, and is a tall, elegant building dating from the Georgian period. Kirk Langley village has some fine, 18th-century stone houses and a mid-17th-century, gabled, red-brick rectory. The parish church of St Michael dates from the 14th century and has a fine Perpendicular tower and interesting heraldic glass and tiles. The screen under the tower is said to be one of the oldest timber screens in Derbyshire. There are many memorials to the ruling Meynell family in the church, and a much-loved former vicar is remembered in the Leeke Memorial Hall, which was the village school until 1879 and is now the centre of many village activities.

KNIVETON (Derbyshire Dales)

SK2050: 3 miles (5km) NE of Ashbourne

The name has nothing to do with knives, but refers to a Saxon named

Cengifu who first built a farm here. Kniveton is a pretty, stone-built village between Ashbourne and Carsington, on the slopes of Madge Hill. The **parish church of St Michael** has a stumpy 13th-century spire and a Norman south doorway with what appears to be a bear carved in the keystone. The varnished wooden pews and gallery and chancel windows all belong to a severe 18th-century restoration. The arms of the local Kniveton family, Royalists who became impoverished during the Civil War, are preserved in the windows of the chancel, and there is an ornate 18th-century monument to Greenwood Holmes, erected by his nephew.

Across the fields to the north of the village is the hilltop Bronze Age burial mound of **Wigber Low**, which has revealed important remains from that period.

LITTLE EATON (Erewash)

SK3641: 3 miles (5km) N of Derby

Little Eaton is a pretty village of stone-built cottages on three sides of its green and views across the River Derwent to the hills beyond Duffield. It has expanded quickly in recent years as a commuter village serving nearby Derby, but in the 1920s and 30s it was a popular weekend resort for the people of that city. For the price of a train trip, they could enjoy the lovely surroundings of the village or take a twopenny canal ride on the Derby Canal to Coxbench Wood.

A well-remembered 'character' of those days was Alice Grace – 'the Little Eaton Hermit' – who was evicted from a cottage behind the Queen's Head pub-lic house for non-payment of rent. The cottage has since been demolished. She lived for twenty years in various sheds and barns before taking up residence in her famous 'box homes' at the pinfold at 'Th' Back o' the Winns' in Coxbench Wood. Alice became a local personality and many postcards were sold of her. She died in the Shardlow Workhouse in 1927 and is buried in an unmarked grave at the little **parish church of St Paul.** The Victorian Norman-style building has an embattled tower, and took the place of a Georgian church built in 1791.

Little Eaton ought to be remembered as one of the birthplaces of the Railway Age, for in 1793, Benjamin Outram of Butterley Hall invented the flanged rail. He then laid one of the earliest railways in the world, which ran from Denby to Little Eaton. Four horses pulled eight wooden-wheeled trucks laden with coal, and for over a century, until its closure in 1908, coal trains were hauled along the so-called 'gang railway' to be unloaded into narrow boats at the Canal Wharf on the Derby Canal at Little Eaton. All that remains of this now is the **Canal Clockhouse**, which stands defiantly still ticking away the hours among modern industrial units.

LITTLE LONGSTONE (Derbyshire Dales)

SK187: 3 miles (5km) NW of Bakewell

This tiny hamlet is on the minor road between Great Longstone and Monsal Head, one of the most popular viewpoints in the Peak District National Park. The view from outside the strangely Bavarian-style **Monsal Head Hotel** looks out over the graceful, five-arched **Monsal Head Viaduct**, built as part of the Midland Line. It ran north into Upper Dale and west down Monsal Dale, with the impressive, Iron Age hill fort of **Fin Cop** dominating the scene.

The building of the Midland Line through Monsal Dale in 1863 was the cause of one of John Ruskin's most famous outbursts. In his *Fors Clavigera*, Volume 1, he fumed: 'There was a rocky valley between Buxton and Bakewell, once upon a time, divine as the Vale of Tempe...You Enterprised a Railroad through the valley – you blasted its rocks away, heaped thousands of tons of shale into its lovely stream. The valley is gone, and the Gods with it; and now, every fool in Buxton can be at Bakewell in half an hour, and every fool in Bakewell at Buxton.'

Now, of course, the viaduct is a protected structure and very much part of the Monsal Head scene, forming part of the National Park's **Monsal Trail** walking and riding route. There are long-term plans for the restoration of a steam railway to the line, so the ghost of Ruskin may still rise to haunt the developers.

Little Longstone is perhaps best known today for its tiny but welcoming 16th-century **Pack Horse Inn**, much beloved of walkers on the Monsal Trail. But the Victorian rustic-Gothic Church of England Chapel standing in a field at the western end of the village has many admirers, and the 17th-century **Manor House** standing behind its yew hedges in the centre of the hamlet was the home of the Longsdon family for twenty-eight generations.

LITTLEOVER (Derby)
SK3234: 2 miles (3km) SW of Derby

Littleover, once a pleasant village on the outskirts of Derby, has now largely been overtaken by the creeping suburban growth of that city. The multi-gabled **parish church of St Peter** has a Norman western doorway, but most of the rest, apart from the 14th-century chancel, was over-restored in the 19th century. There is a fine coloured monument to Sir Richard Harpur, who died in 1635 and who is shown in a flowing gown kneeling at a prayer desk opposite his wife, with their six children beneath. The Harpur family lived at the old hall in the village, and boasted that they supplied more High Sheriffs for the county than any other.

LITTON (Derbyshire Dales)
SK1674: 4 miles (6km) NW of Bakewell

In many ways, Litton, a small village 1000ft (300m) up on the limestone plateau, is a typical White Peak village. Clustered around its long village green with an ancient cross at one end, the range of stone-built cottages, mainly dating from the 17th and 18th centuries, is as pretty as a picture, and as a result, is frequently photographed. The Red Lion public house is a popular hostelry at the centre of the village, where the stocks still stand on the green. Much of Litton's prosperity was built on the traditional dual industries of lead mining and farming, of which only farming now remains as an important employer of local labour. The combined school, church and library was built by Canon Samuel Andrews, Vicar of nearby Tideswell, in 1865, and a more modern church was built in

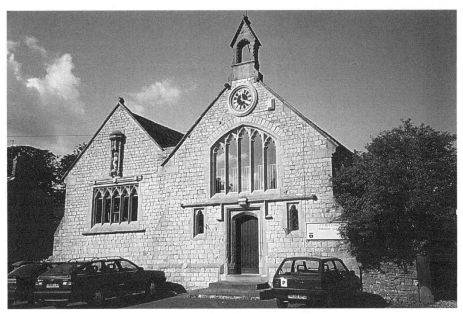

Primary school, Litton, built in 1835

1929. Litton hosts a popular well-dressing in June each year. Down in the dale is **Litton Mill**, an early cotton mill built in 1782 and now being converted to holiday and living accommodation. This was the scene, if the propagandist *Memoirs of Robert Blincoe* of 1828 are to be believed, where the owner, Ellis Needham, perpetrated some of the worst examples of child exploitation in the 19th century. Whatever the truth, the *Memoirs* were a potent catalyst towards long-overdue factory reforms.

One of Litton's most famous sons was William Bagshawe, the so-called 'Apostle of the Peak', who was an outstanding Nonconformist preacher in this land of Nonconformism, and is buried at Chapel-en-le-Frith.

LONG EATON (Erewash)

SK4933: 8 miles (13km) E of Derby

Once a self-contained village at the junction of three counties, Derbyshire, Nottinghamshire and Leicestershire; and four rivers, the Trent, Derwent, Erewash and Soar, Long Eaton has now joined Stapleford and Beeston as one of the vast suburbs of nearby Nottingham. In the old days, the important village was Sawley, down by the Trent, but Long Eaton has long since assumed greater importance, especially since the coming of the railway and the enormous railway sidings for which the place was famous.

What you see of the **parish church of St Laurence,** just behind the Market Place in the centre of the town, is mainly a 19th-century rebuilding, with its recessed spire standing on an ashlar-faced tower. The old nave, now the south aisle, has a Norman doorway with beakhead mouldings, and there are fragmentary remains of other Norman work in the restored church. Other churches include the brick-built St John the Evangelist in College Street, dating from 1916, and the Wesley Reform Church in Derby Road. The buildings and playing fields of **Trent College**, built in 1866-8, dominate the town. The College Chapel was built in 1874 to designs by Robinson of Derby, but extensively remodelled internally by A.E. Richardson in 1949.

Trent Lock, where the Leicestershire Soar joins the Trent and Mersey Canal, is a popular place of resort for the residents of Long Eaton, and is usually alive with pleasure craft.

LONGFORD
(Derbyshire Dales)

SK2137: 9 miles (14km) W of Derby

At first sight, the name of the village pub in Longford – *The Ostrich* – might raise some eyebrows. In fact, the choice of the large, flightless bird comes not from some exotic local farming practices, but from the coat of arms of the Coke family, lords of the manor here since the early 17th century, and owners of the handsome, brick manor house of **Longford Hall**. Originally built as a Tudor mansion by the de Longford family who settled here in the 13th century, Longford Hall was extensively remodelled in 1700, giving us the present balustraded and buttressed house, where the four projecting buttresses double as chimneys. The hall, which is private, stands in its own grounds, which are decorated with stately limes and yews.

There are many alabaster memorials to the de Longford and Cokes (relations of the Earls of Leicester) in the **parish church of St Chad**, near the hall. The earliest of which is probably that of Sir Nicholas Longford, who died in 1357.

There are traces of the original Norman church in the present building, but the spacious chancel dates from the 14th century and the fine, ashlar-faced west tower from a century later.

The **Pump House**, once the main source of water for the village, stands in the centre of Longford, on the corner of Long Lane. The village school also serves the villages of Hollington, Alkmonton and Rodsley. The mill, first mentioned in the 11th century but rebuilt in 1837, is now a private house and the machinery has been handed over to the Arkwright Society at Cromford. The former cheese factory, now a farm store, stands opposite the old mill.

MACKWORTH (Amber Valley)

SK3137: 3 miles (5km) W of Derby

Only the front wall of the turreted 15th-century gatehouse remains of what was once the mighty **Mackworth Castle**, home of the Mackworth family, who served under the Black Prince at Poitiers. The castle was destroyed during the Civil War. This prosperous village on the outskirts of Derby remains surprisingly intact as the main street is off the busy main A52 Derby-Ashbourne road.

The beautiful old **parish church of All Saints** stands back from the road, isolated in a field to the east of the village centre. Its tall Perpendicular tower and spire date from the early 14th century. There are persistent stories that the massive tower once had a defensive purpose, but there is no evidence that this was the case, except for its external appearance. The interior of the church was much modified by the Victorians, and now presents a lavish, over-the-top example of their love of decoration. A good instance of this is the extraordinarily exuberant lectern, dated 1903.

A footpath leads across the fields from the church to the tiny hamlet of **Markeaton** on the outskirts of Derby, which is dominated by the massive Derby Crematorium and its grounds.

On the opposite, southern, side of the A52 is the massive Mackworth Housing Estate, built immediately after the war to house Derby's overspill. It has little connection with the village whose name it took.

MAPPERLEY (Amber Valley)

SK4343: 2 miles (3km) NW of Ilkeston

The small, former mining village of Mapperley stands on crossroads at the southern edge of the large **Shipley Country Park**, which now includes the large and hugely popular **American Adventure Theme Park**. But its history begins long ago. It was granted a charter to hold a fair and market as long ago as 1267, but little remains of those days.

The **parish church of the Holy Trinity** stands on a hill to the south of the village and was erected in 1851. It was badly affected by mining subsidence from the nearby Mapperley Colliery, which closed in 1966. In the same year, the new, rebuilt church was opened, and is of a novel design, incorporating the ancient principle of cruck framing. Much use has been made of plain glass in the western gable and in the north windows, which command a fine view to the south. Appropriately, mining scenes are featured in the stained glass

of the west door. The Methodist Chapel opened in 1875, but is now a private house. To the north of the village, the reservoir in Mapperley Park has a popular picnic area on its banks.

MAPPLETON (Derbyshire Dales)

SK1648: 2 miles (3km) NW of Ashbourne

The roof of the little **parish church of St Mary** at Mappleton comes as a bit of a shock in this land of sturdy, stone-built church towers. Dubbed 'Little St Paul's' it is crowned by an octagonal dome with a lantern. The church was built of stone in the 18th century. Most of the older houses in the rest of this pretty little village in the valley of the Dove are of the red brick of the Midlands, as opposed to the stone of the Peak. Typical of these is the **Clergymen's Widows' Almshouses**, just to the west of the church. This handsome, five-bay, brick house of 1727 has stone dressings and a hipped roof. The centre bay projects and is framed by gigantic rusticated pilasters. The **Manor House**, overlooking the water-meadows of the River Dove south of the village, is another good 18th-century brick building.

MARSTON MONTGOMERY (Derbyshire Dales)

SK1338: 6 miles (10km) SW of Ashbourne

The aristocratic, double-barrelled name refers to the Montgomery family, who owned land in Marston and nearby Cubley at the time of the Domesday Book. Lying in a quiet corner of the county, between the A515 and the A50, Marston enjoys fine views to the west towards the Weaver Hills of Staffordshire – the last of the Pennines. There are a number of old houses in the village, some of which are agricultural barns that have been converted to residential use. One which has gone in the opposite direction is the half-timbered **Manor Farm**, formerly the Manor House, in the centre of the village. There is another fine old farmhouse dated 1632 in the attached hamlet of Waldey, and many of the surrounding dairy farms have 17th-century farmhouses.

The **parish church of St Giles** has a low, sloping roof, and a pyramidal bellcot dating from 1875. But the rest of the church, although thoroughly restored in the 19th century, has much early Norman work on show, including the south doorway with its tympanum, the chancel arch, and the font. The windows in the raised chancel are late 13th century. The village school, built in the centre of the village in 1872, takes pupils from Cubley as well as Marston.

MARSTON-ON-DOVE (South Derbyshire)

SK2329: 9 miles (14km) SW of Derby

The little 13th-century **parish church of St Mary**, with its fine Decorated spire watching over the water-meadows of the Dove, has several claims to fame. Inside the ashlar-faced, 14th-century west tower resides the oldest bell in Derbyshire. It was cast by John de Stafford at Leicester in 1366 and is inscribed with the words 'Hail Mary'. The vicar's list shows that the

church had only four incumbents for nearly 200 years between 1685 and 1876. The first two of these preached for 119 years from the simple oak pulpit – which must be something of a record. The church organ was brought from nearby Sudbury Hall for £74 in 1827 – before that accompaniment was by a small orchestra.

Marston-on-Dove was owned by the monks of nearby Tutbury Abbey at the time of Domesday, but reverted to Henry de Ferrers when Norman rule began. Today, the tiny hamlet consists of a handful of cottages and three farms. Most of the more modern housing is in the neighbouring hamlet of Hilton.

MATLOCK (Derbyshire Dales)

SK3060: 15 miles (24km) N of Derby

It is entirely appropriate that Derbyshire County Council should have its headquarters in the busy, mid-Derbyshire town of Matlock. The name of the place comes from the Old English 'Meslach' and probably means 'the oak where the moot was held'. It would seem, therefore, that local government has been administered from this place on the River Derwent ('the river of oaks') for over 900 years.

John Smedley's huge **Hydro**, where the County Council now meets, still lords it over the town from the Matlock Bank hillside where it was built in 1853. It is an amazing building – from the front (south), with its terraced gardens (now mainly a car park for county council employees) and central domed tower topped with an ironwork corona, it looks like nothing less than an enormous seaside hotel. But the building at the rear, linked by a covered bridge across Smedley Street, is more like a grim industrial factory. Smedley was the man who founded modern Matlock, promoting it as a centre for the then-fashionable cure of hydrotherapy, which involved all kinds of showers and other bathing contraptions and the appliance of copious amounts of spring water at various temperatures.

Nearby is **All Saints Church**, which was built in 1883. It has a beautiful William Morris and Company east window by Burne-Jones, dating from 1905. Patients reached the Hydro up the very steep Bank Road and Rutland Street by cable-hauled tramcars. It was said to be the steepest tramway on a public road in the world and the Matlock trams became quite a famous tourist attraction. They ran safely for thirty-four years, until the lines were taken up in 1927. The decorative tramway shelter, surmounted by a clock, still stands in the riverside Public Gardens.

Smedley built the fairy-tale but now ruinous **Riber Castle** for himself. It overlooks the town in most views from its prominent hilltop to the south. Smedley's initiative attracted others, and at the turn of the century there were over twenty hydropathic establishments in the town. Another, the Wyvern House Hydro, became the Ernest Bailey Comprehensive School.

No less than eight hamlets make up the modern town of Matlock, including the original settlement of **Old Matlock**, on the hillside to the east of the river, where a charming 18th-century rectory can be found next to the former Wheatsheaf Farm, which dates from 1681.

The **parish church of St Giles** in Old Matlock has a 15th-century Perpendicular tower, but most of the rest was rebuilt in the 19th century. The font, however, is Norman. Six paper 'maidens' crants', or garlands, hang in the church, commemorating girls who died before marriage *(see Ashford-in-the-Water).*

Matlock Bridge, over the powerful River Derwent, dates from the 15th century, but has been widened to take modern traffic. Crown Square, topped by its somewhat incongruous, modern stainless steel 'crown' in the middle of the roundabout by the bridge, is the centre of the modern town. The main shopping area is in Dale Road, which leads to Matlock Bath.

MATLOCK BATH (Derbyshire Dales)

SK2958: 1 mile (2km) S of Matlock

Matlock Bath on a summer Sunday is the Blackpool of the Peak District. It has become a popular destination for motorcyclists, and the bikers can be seen sunning themselves and admiring each other's machines along the South Parade by the river.

The town has been tourist trap since the health-giving properties of its warm springs were discovered in the late 17th century. The original attraction may have been the lime and salt-rich solutions from the springs, which coat anything with which they come into contact with a rock known as tufa. The Wishing Well near the Temple Road car park is a good example.

Matlock Bath occupies the bottom of the steep-sided **Derwent Gorge**, with the great 300ft (90m) limestone shield of **High Tor** overshadowing everything. This is a popular resort of serious rock-climbers, who can often be seen hanging, apparently precariously, from its smooth, blank wall of rock. On the other side of the river, the wooded slopes of the **Heights of Abraham** (named after General Wolfe's famous Quebec battle) can be reached much more easily, but just as spectacularly, by the cable cars. These swing up from the Joseph Paxton's Swiss chalet-style former Matlock Bath Station, now the **Whistlestop** Centre of the Derbyshire Wildlife Trust, to the **Victoria Tower**, which marks the summit.

The **Great Rutland and Masson Caverns** are former lead mines that have been opened up to allow visitors to enjoy the underground splendours of the caves which riddle the Heights of Abraham. The **Royal Cave** and **Temple Mine** are former fluorspar workings which are also open to visitors. They are near the fascinating **Peak District Mining Museum**, which is housed with the Tourist Information Centre in **The Pavilion**, originally built in 1885 for the spa trade. The major exhibit in the museum is the large water-pressure engine, dated 1819, which was rescued from a local lead mine. There are also replica shafts and tunnels for children to climb and crawl through, among a host of other interesting exhibits. The **New Bath** Hotel on the A6, where John Ruskin stayed in 1829, also dates from the period of Matlock Bath's prominence as a spa. So too does the elegant spire of the **parish church of the Holy Trinity**, which was built in 1842. But the most beautiful piece of ecclesiastical architecture in Matlock Bath is the little hillside **Chapel of St**

John the Baptist on Cliff Road, high above the village. This was built in 1897, to a design by Sir Guy Dawber, as a chapel of ease, and its medieval-looking turrets and oriel windows are matched inside by a rood screen, reredos, and exuberantly painted walls.

The coming of the railway to Matlock Bath in 1849 gave a great boost to its emerging tourist industry, and the line still connects to the main line at Derby, fourteen miles away.

MELBOURNE
(South Derbyshire)

SK3825: 8 miles (13km) S of Derby

Melbourne's **parish church of St Michael and St Mary** is widely regarded as one of the finest Norman parish churches in the country. The external view, with incomplete twin Norman west towers with 19th-century roofs no higher than the nave roof, gives no clue to the magnificent and beautifully preserved interior. But when you step inside you can only marvel at the forest of tall circular columns in the six-bay nave, all thickly decorated with zigzag moulding, and the clerestory and wall passage above. The crossing at the junction of the nave and chancel is especially stunning, and the chancel was originally finished with an apse. The whole effect is more like one of the great cathedrals – such as Durham – or collegiate churches than a mere parish church. Pevsner believed that most of Melbourne's details dated from the 12th century, although the plan may have been drawn up before 1100. The present square east end is late 15th century, and the upper part of the tower is

Norman west door, Melbourne Parish
Church

early 17th. The west front, although never completed, also has a wealth of Norman details.

The reason for what Pevsner dubbed 'one of the most ambitious Norman parish churches of England' goes back to 1133, when Henry I granted the manor and rectory of Melbourne to Adelulph, the first Bishop of Carlisle, when the see was founded. At the time, Melbourne lay on the edge of the heathen north, and after Carlisle had been sacked by the Scots, the bishop conducted much of his business from Melbourne.

Nothing remains of the once mighty **Melbourne Castle**, which was granted

a licence to crenellate in 1311 and was visited by King John on several occasions. It was a large structure with many towers, but was dismantled by 1460 and now only a single wall stands behind Castle Farm, a partly 17th-century brick house.

There are a number of other good 17th- and 18th-century brick buildings in Melbourne's pretty village centre, which is dominated by Melbourne Pool, close to the south entrance of **Melbourne Hall**, originally the residence of the Bishops of Carlisle. In the early 17th century, the house was leased to Sir John Coke, who later bought it and began the transformation to the rather forbidding stone building of today. The south front, with its deep recesses, was built in 1725 by Francis Smith, and the decorative east, or garden, front by William Smith in 1744. It was Thomas Coke, Sir John's great-grandson, who had the lovely Melbourne Hall gardens laid out 'to suit with Versailles' by the royal gardeners, London and Wise in 1696. Lawns lead down to the large pool, across which stands Robert Bakewell's wonderfully ornate wrought-iron Arbour or Birdcage. There is also a long tunnel of ancient clipped yews, a rocky grotto with a wishing well, and many decorative figures and monuments of lead. The house went by marriage to the Lamb family, and when Peniston Lamb was created a peer in 1770, he took the title of Lord Melbourne. His son, the second Lord Melbourne, became Queen Victoria's first Prime Minister, and the Australian city of Melbourne was named after him. The present owner of Melbourne Hall is the Marquis of Lothian. It is occasionally open to the public, who can admire the delightful mainly 17th- and 18th-century interiors.

Apart from the residents of the 'big house', Melbourne also lays claim to being the birthplace, in 1808, of the man who brought cheap holiday travel to all. **Thomas Cook** was born in a cottage (now demolished) in Quick Close, at the top of the High Street. He was a gardener, wood-turner and local missionary before setting up as a tourist agent in Leicester. His first organised trip was to take 570 passengers on the Midland Railway from Leicester to Loughborough and back in 1841 for a fare of one shilling (5p) each. Thomas was joined by his son, John, who at the age of 17, conveyed 165,000 to London to see the Great Exhibition of 1851. Thomas died in 1892, having established his company as the pioneer of popular travel.

Contained within the parish of Melbourne is the pretty village of King's Newton, of which **The Hall** is the principal building. It stands on the site of the Elizabethan manor which was burned down in 1859, and was rebuilt by Cecil Paget in the Tudor style in 1910. The former lords of the manor were the Hardinge family, remembered in the name of the Hardinge Arms public house, across the road from the hall. It was here that a former landlord, William Taylor, first bred, apparently by accident, the 'Newton Wonder' apple.

MICKLEOVER
(South Derbyshire)

SK3034: 3 miles (5km) SW of Derby

Now not much more than a dormitory town for nearby Derby, Mickleover is still known as 'the village' to its older residents. The old market place, known as The Square, still remains to remind the visitor of its ancient past, with its green and the older houses in Hollow Street and Orchard Street. Western Lane, once known as Poke Lane, also still has two older cottages. The oldest building in the village however, is the **Old Hall**, a timber-framed, two-gabled building with brick infilling. Oliver Cromwell is said to have stayed here when he stormed Tutbury Castle during the Civil War.

The **parish church of All Saints** is early 14th century, but suffered an over-zealous Victorian restoration, as so many Derbyshire churches did, in 1858. In 1945, the original 14th-century font was found and restored to its original position, and is in regular use by the expanding population of the village to this day. The modern Anglican **church of St John** was built in the 1960s, and the original village school, built in 1881, has become the village community centre.

MIDDLETON-BY-WIRKSWORTH
(Derbyshire Dales)

SK2755: 1 mile (2km) NW of Wirksworth

Mining and quarrying have been important planks of the local economy in this part of Derbyshire for hundreds of years, and the enormous and impressive Hopton Wood Quarries, south of the village, are still producing limestone, as they have for many years. So it was entirely appropriate that the **National Stone Centre** should be set up recently in a disused quarry south of

Middleton and adjacent to the High Peak Trail, formerly the Cromford and High Peak Railway. Close by is the Middleton Top Engine House on the Trail, which was used to haul waggons up the 1:8 gradient of the Middleton Incline. The steam engine used to haul the waggons has been restored and is often 'in steam' at weekends in the summer. The National Stone Centre tells the important story of stone in the Peak District landscape – from fossils to quarrying, and visitors can even pan for gems in one of the hands-on exhibits.

The village of Middleton has a number of good old stone cottages, especially around the Jail Yard, which is a reminder that Middleton was a place of correction for miscreant lead miners in the past. The **parish church of the Holy Trinity** was built in 1844, but is somewhat overshadowed by the Congregational Chapel which was built by a Matlock Bath minister to serve the needs of Middleton's large number of lead miners.

D.H. Lawrence spent a year at the small house known as **Mountain Cottage**, overlooking the Via Gellia (see BONSALL). It is thought that the village of 'Woodlinkin' in his novel *The Virgin and the Gypsy* was based on Middleton-by-Wirksworth.

MIDDLETON-BY-YOULGREAVE (Derbyshire Dales)

SK1963: 4 miles (6km) SW of Bakewell

Centred on the broad open space of The Square, this charming little village above Bradford Dale was once the home of the Fulwood family. Nothing now remains of their castle except a mound and a few ivy-covered walls behind Castle Farm. Sir Christopher Fulwood supported the King during the troubled times of the Civil War, and when his home was raided by Roundheads, he hid in a rock crevice in the dale. He was discovered and shot. **Lomberdale Hall**, a Victorian mansion halfway between Middleton and Youlgreave, was the home of the **William and Thomas Bateman**, the leading antiquarians and pioneer archaeologists of their day. Between them they excavated most of Derbyshire and the Peak District's prehistoric burial mounds, carefully recording and collecting what they found. When Thomas Bateman died in 1861, the outstanding family collection of artefacts was transferred to the Weston Park Museum in Sheffield, where it can still be seen. Thomas Bateman's grave, ornamented with a replica Bronze Age collared burial urn, can be found behind the former **Congregational Chapel**, built in the centre of the village in 1828 by his grandfather. Almost opposite is the substantial, twin-gabled Square House, formerly a public house known as the Bateman Arms.

Two miles to the west on Middleton Common lies the most famous and impressive prehistoric site in Derbyshire, sometimes dubbed 'the Stonehenge of the North'. The **Arbor Low** henge and stone circle (English Heritage), together with the attendant burial mounds, were thoroughly investigated by **Thomas Bateman**. Nevertheless, the origin and purpose of the circular earthwork and ditch, with its circle of fifty fallen limestone monoliths, still remain a mystery. Current thinking is that it must have been some kind of important sacred or ritual site for the people of the Neolithic age, who built it nearly 5000 years ago. Standing at 1230ft (375m) above the sea, it commands a wonderful panorama of the White Peak plateau, in which almost every high point is topped by a 'low' – usually a burial mound from the Bronze Age, and nearly all excavated by Thomas Bateman during his assiduous archaeological campaigns. Archaeologists are now agreed that the massive stones of the Arbor Low circle must originally have stood vertically, just like their more famous contemporaries on Salisbury Plain. A Bronze Age burial mound also excavated by Bateman is superimposed on the south-eastern rim of the henge, and a couple of fields away lies the massive tumulus of **Gib Hill**, which consists of another Bronze Age round barrow superimposed on a Neolithic long barrow beneath.

MILFORD (Amber Valley)

SK3445: 6 miles (10km) N of Derby

The power of the River Derwent brought Jedediah Strutt to Milford, where he built the mill which gave the village its name around 1780. Nothing remains of his original building, but the splendid clock which once called the apprentices to work is in Derby Museum and the fortress-like, windowless walls of his later mill still stand by the Derwent Bridge. This handsome bridge was built in 1790 with two elegant segmented arches, and still carries the constant roaring traffic on the A6. Strutt lived at **Milford House**, a fine, seven-bay, stone house. A former gritstone quarry in the centre of the village, by

the side of the A6, has been converted into a children's playground.

The **parish church of the Holy Trinity** was built in the Early English style by Moffat, a partner of Sir George Gilbert Scott, in 1848.

MILLER'S DALE (Derbyshire Dales)

SK1373: 5 miles (8km) E of Buxton

The presence of the two cast-iron railway bridges which now carry the **Monsal Trail** give the only clue to this tiny hamlet's former importance. When the Midland Line was constructed in the 1860s, following the valley of the River Wye and through some of the most difficult country in Britain, Miller's Dale became the junction for the fast expanding spa town of Buxton. Some of the railwaymen's cottages still survive down by the river, and the former station has been converted to a Ranger Briefing Centre and car park for the National Park Authority. Also by the river is the 19th-century former corn mill, now a private house, which gave the hamlet its name.

The **parish church of St Anne** was built in 1880 in the Victorian Gothic style by Canon Samuel Andrew of Tideswell. The railway closed in 1967 and was converted to the Monsal Trail walking and riding route. Parts of it, including a former limestone quarry down the line from the station, are now managed by the Derbyshire Wildlife Trust as a nature reserve, and the towering limekilns just down the line from the station, which emptied their products straight into railway waggons beneath, have been restored to their former condition. Lime was an important local commodity for many years, and the presence of the railway made its export easy.

Upstream along the trail are the tremendous limestone buttresses of **Chee Dale**, a favourite haunt of rock-climbers.

MONYASH (Derbyshire Dales)

SK1566: 4 miles (6km) W of Bakewell

This small, attractive village at the head of beautiful **Lathkill Dale** (part of the Derbyshire Dales National Nature Reserve) was granted its charter to hold a weekly market as long ago as 1340. The stump of the ancient **market cross** remains, on the spacious village green opposite the 17th-century **Bull's Head** public house, but the market went long ago.

Monyash was founded on the high and dry White Peak limestone plateau because of the presence of its 'meres' – ponds which owe their existence to a bed of impervious clay which held the precious water. Only Fere Mere, on the road towards Buxton, now remains, and the site of Jack Mere has been converted to a car park by the National Park Authority. The **parish church of St Leonard** dates from the 12th century, and is one of the prettiest in the county. The elegant spire rises from a solid, battlemented and unbuttressed tower, and the spacious interior has wide north and south transepts. Among its treasures is an enormous iron-bound parish chest, which may date as far back as the 13th century. Monyash became a centre of the Quaker movement in the late 18th century, when its importance as the site

of a Barmote Court for the lead mining industry was at its height. Many of the local fields are still dotted with old lead mining shafts, and at Ricklow, at the head of Lathkill Dale, a flourishing 'marble' quarry existed in Victorian times. (The marble was, in fact, a highly polished fossiliferous limestone.)

One Ash Grange, above the deep ravine of Lathkill Dale, was originally a penitentiary for recalcitrant monks and later the home of John Gratton, a prominent Quaker preacher, and is now the site of one of the National Park's network of camping barns.

MORLEY (Erewash)

SK3941: 5 miles (8km) NE of Derby

The great glory of Morley is the magnificent **parish church of St Matthew,** which is one of the most interesting and important in the county. It has one of the finest displays of late medieval stained glass in the county, and its collection of medieval monuments is unrivalled and on the scale of a small cathedral. The nave of the church is Norman, and the tower, chancel and north chapel are late 14th and early 15th century. But it is the detail of the interior which is so stunning. The monuments and brasses to the Statham, Sacheverell and Sitwell families date from 1453. They include those of John Sacheverell who died at Bosworth Field in 1485, and the beautifully carved tomb chest of Henry Sacheverell (died 1558) and his wife Katherine Babington (1543), which according to Pevsner 'might well be in Westminster Abbey'. Much of the stained glass in the church came from Dale Abbey at the Dissolution of the Monasteries, and at least three windows in the north chancel chapel and the north windows are filled with original medieval glass dating from 1482. The glass was sensitively restored and added to in 1847.

Morley village is really a series of detached hamlets, the centre of which is the Church Lane area nearest the church. **Morley Manor**, on the main road, is a mock-Tudor house built for the Sacheverell-Batemans in 1900, and the tithe barn, behind the church, was regularly used for village festivals such as harvest suppers. Between Almshouses Lane and the church is Morley's mysterious mound. Now tree-covered, it may have been the site of the 'Morlestone' mentioned in the Domesday Book of 1086, and it appears to be some kind of moated defensive site. The disused brickworks in Brick Kiln Lane is now a nature reserve managed by the Derbyshire Wildlife Trust.

The **Derbyshire Agricultural College** is at Broomfield Hall, south of the village, where there is also a golf course in the Green Belt between the village and Derby.

MUGGINTON (Amber Valley)

SK2843: 6 miles (10km) NW of Derby

The rather strange name comes from the Old English and is thought to mean 'the farm of Mogga or Mugga', an unknown Saxon who farmed here before the Normans came. Farming is still the predominant industry in Mugginton, a straggling village above the Mercaston Brook, off the Derby-Ashbourne road. The **parish church of All Saints,** at the

southern end of the village, has a sturdy Norman tower with a lovely Norman arch inside and a Perpendicular south chancel chapel. There are good brass monuments on a tomb chest to Nicholas Kniveton and his wife (1475). The Kniveton family lived at neighbouring Mercaston, across the brook of the same name, where the old Hall survives as a farmhouse. The last of the line, Sir Andrew Kniveton, was impoverished by the Civil War and sold the house in 1654.

A mile and a half to the north-west stands the mysterious **Halter Devil Chapel**, a small, stone-faced building attached to a farmhouse, which was constructed in 1723 but enlarged in 1890. The legend attached to this odd building is that Francis Brown, a farmer, resolved to set out one stormy night to Derby, saying he would go even if he had to 'halter the Devil himself'. When he went to find his horse in a field, he discovered to his horror that it had grown horns and a flash of lightning convinced him it was the Devil. When he recovered, he repented his rash vow, and endowed the chapel.

NETHERSEAL (South Derbyshire)

SK2813: 4 miles (6km) S of Swadlincote

Standing on the borders of Derbyshire, Staffordshire, Leicestershire and Warwickshire, Netherseal overlooks the River Mease in pleasant wooded countryside off the main Burton-upon-Trent to Nuneaton road. The mainly rebuilt **parish church of St Peter** has a fine Perpendicular tower and 13th century nave. In the chancel is a carved stone slab memorial to Roger Doulton, a rector of the church who died in 1500. There are other memorials to the Gresley family, the most famous of which was Sir Nigel Gresley, chief mechanical engineer to the London and North Eastern Railway and designer of the famous Coronation and Silver Jubilee Pacific class locomotives. An even more famous engine was later named after him. He was the grandson of the Reverend Sir Nigel Gresley, the 9th Baronet, the Rector of Seal, and is buried in the churchyard under an oak supposedly descended from the Boscobel Oak in Staffordshire.

NEW MILLS (High Peak)

SK0085: 3 miles (5km) N of Whaley Bridge

The 'new mills' which gave this industrial township its name were the cotton mills which sprang up here, at the junction of the River Sett with the Goyt, in the later years of the 19th century. Until it became a united parish under the name of New Mills in 1884, there were a series of small hamlets known as Ollersett, Beard, Thornsett and Whittle. **Ollerset Hall**, at Low Leighton, is a gabled and mullioned 17th-century manor house, once at the centre of a separate hamlet. Few of the mills which gave the town its name are left today, but New Mills still has a busy, industrial look about it. The soaring stone viaducts and bridges which span the picturesque and surprisingly deep little gorge of the Goyt – known as **The Torrs** – as it passes through the town are a constant reminder of that industrial past. Recent improvements have greatly enhanced the scenic beauty of this unexpectedly spectacular spot, and the proximity of the converted railway line known as the Sett Valley Trail, which runs from here to Hayfield (see HAYFIELD), provides another recreational opportunity for townsfolk.

St George's Parish Church in Church Road was built in 1831 in the Early English style, and **St James the Less**, with its attached almshouses, in 1880 by Swinden Barber. It was built as a memorial to the local philanthropist, James Ingham. But this is Nonconformist country, and it is the chapels, such as the Congregational Providence Chapel in Mellor Road (1823) and the Methodist Chapel in St George Road (1810) which answered most of the spiritual needs of the millworkers. Their temporal needs have been answered by the Bull's Head public house in the High Street since the 18th century.

In the hills to the north of New Mills is the tiny and picturesque gritstone hamlet of **Rowarth**, sheltering beneath Lantern Pike. North of Rowarth, on the summit of Cown Edge, are a pair of round pillars known as **Robin Hood's Picking Rods**. No one is sure exactly when or what they were built for, but tradition claims they were used by the legendary outlaw for bending and stringing his bows.

NEWTON SOLNEY (South Derbyshire)

SK2825: 2 miles (3km) NE of Burton-upon-Trent

Newton Solney stands on high ground overlooking the confluence of Derbyshire's River Dove with the mighty Trent, just outside Burton-upon-Trent.

It takes its name from the de Solney, or Sulney, family, which was granted land here in the reign of Henry III.

The Norman **parish church of St Mary** is reached by passing the quaint, octagonal **Beehive Cottage,** down a tree-lined lane towards the river. It has a stumpy little spire rising from an equally short tower. The interior of this charming church is mostly 14th century, with Perpendicular chancel windows and clerestory. There is a fascinating collection of monuments, many to medieval members of the de Solney family, including a headless knight of the mid-13th century and an alabaster, cross-legged knight of around 1375. The impressive, semi-reclining marble figure of Sir Henry Every, 3rd Baronet of Eggington, who died in 1709, is dressed in flowing Roman robes. In the churchyard, overlooking the river, is the tombstone of Thomas Gayfere, the master mason who was responsible for the restoration of Westminster Hall and Henry VII's Chapel in London. He died in 1827.

Half a mile west of the village on a wooded hill stand the romantic, castellated red-brick ruins of **Bladon Castle,** built in the early 19th century by Sir Jeffrey Wyatville for a Mr Hoskins of Newton Park. Known as Hoskins' Folly, it was built as an eye-catcher, but later served as a house. It was commandeered by the army during the war, and was later used as a prisoner of war camp.

NORBURY (Derbyshire Dales)
SK1242: 5 miles (8km) SW of Ashbourne

Norbury's **parish church of St Mary and St Barlok** is one of the most interesting and beautiful in Derbyshire. Tucked away down a little lane which leads to the River Dove and surrounded by trees, the church, with its curiously truncated, central tower and superb Decorated 14th-century chancel with ancient stained glass windows, makes a perfect picture. The great east window was carefully restored over a period of ten years and completed in 1983. Most of the glass in it dates from the end of the 14th century, and therefore comprises one of the most important and earliest collections in the county. The chancel was built by Henry Kniveton, Rector of Norbury, between 1339 and 1395. The northern aisle of the nave and the chapel east of the tower were added by Nicholas Fitz-

Norbury Parish Church

herbert, who died in 1473, and the pinnacled tower and chapel to the west of it was added by his grandson, John Fitzherbert, who died in 1513. Although the church is small (chancel and nave are only 95ft/29m long), it gives an impression of breadth and grandeur that many larger churches cannot match. There are also fragments of a Saxon cross and fine tracery on the woodwork of the medieval choir stalls.

As might be expected, most of the splendid set of monuments are to the Fitzherbert family. Most notable are the ornate tomb chest alabaster effigies of Nicholas, and Sir Ralph, who died in 1483. In the centre of the chancel is the brass to Sir Anthony, who died in 1583. The Fitzherberts were staunch Roman Catholics (see GRINDLEFORD) and suffered as a result during the Reformation. All that remains of their medieval manor house is the hidden north-east wing of Norbury Hall, to the west of the church. A brick and quoined façade was added in the early 18th century and masks the antiquity of the building, which was the home of the Fitzherberts for 700 years.

Norbury also has links with the popular Victorian novelist **George Eliot**. Her father, Robert Evans, was born in the hamlet of Roston to the south, as was his brother Adam, who became the subject of the novel *Adam Bede*. His cottage is still pointed out in the village. The school he attended, Bartle Massey's, was the original village school on Green Lane, Roston. Roston centres on the area known as the Bull Ring, but whether this name was associated with bull-baiting or a former cattle market is not known.

NORTH WINGFIELD (North East Derbyshire)

SK4064: 4 miles (6km) S of Chesterfield

North Wingfield is another of those east Derbyshire coal towns which seemed to have lost its heart when the collieries, notably Williamthorpe, closed in the 1980s. Many of the residents of this bustling little town midway between Chesterfield and Clay Cross had been employed in the coal industry, and the closure of the pits was a great shock to the local economy. Along with the closure of the railway sidings which served the pits, it also left large areas of derelict land, much of which is now reclaimed. The creation of the **Five Pits Trail** by Derbyshire County Council has provided miles of traffic-free pathways for walking, cycling or horse riding, with conveniently placed picnic sites which command fine views across the slowly healing countryside. Woodlands, ponds and flower-rich meadows have also been created under the scheme, making the Five Pits Trails a haven for wildlife as well.

North Wingfield's history starts long before the coal mines were sunk. At the road junction near the church in the centre of the town stands the base of a weathered old medieval cross which has been used since 1702 as a guidepost, with three sides of its base carved with pointing fingers. **St Lawrence's Parish Church** has a fine, 80ft (24m) high, 14th-century Perpendicular tower. Inside, the beams of the nave and the chancel also date from the same period. There are many medieval monuments inside the church, some dating from the 13th century. They are probably to the local Deincourt family, but unfortunately most are in a poor state of preservation. The Chantry House to the south of the church, founded in 1488, is now the Blue Bell Inn and restaurant. The Rectory is a handsome, five-bay Georgian house with a segmented pediment above the central doorway.

North Wingfield was the birthplace of a pair of famous musicians. **Thomas Greatorex** was born near here in 1758 and became the organist of Carlisle Cathedral at the tender age of 12. He later became the chief professor of the organ at the Royal Academy of Music in London and was for 12 years the organist at Westminster Abbey. **Harry Hopkinson** was born in North Wingfield at the beginning of the 20th century and became a soprano in St Lawrence's church choir. He later became a famous singer and yodeller, known as 'the Great Torrani', and his records were avidly collected. On a humbler note, Alice Barnett ran the local fish and chip shop for 35 years, and was so well thought of that the council was moved to name an old people's bungalow development 'Alice's View' after her.

OCKBROOK (Erewash)

SK4235: 4 miles (6km) E of Derby

Dominating this nucleated and attractive village on the hills above the busy A52 Derby to Nottingham road is the **Moravian Settlement**, which was founded here in 1750. The terrace of delightful, red-brick, Georgian buildings is centred on the pedimented chapel, with its clock face and white-painted cupola, and the adjacent school, founded in 1799. The chapel retains its original wooden organ gallery, with the pulpit opposite. There were separate choir houses for men and women, who had to enter the chapel by separate doors according to the strict segregation rules of the order. The view from this hilltop site is outstanding, extending across the valleys of the Rivers Trent and Soar to the hills of Charnwood Forest in Leicestershire. The Moravians are a Christian sect originating in Germany which had a tremendous influence on John Wesley during his early life. There were great changes in the village following the arrival of the Moravians. Large houses were built and the community on the hill to the west of the village centre increasingly attracted more affluent, middle-class members of society. Before this, the village had been a centre of the textile industry, and some cottages still show the long lines of framework knitters' windows in their upper storeys. One building which still has this distinctive feature is the **Cross Keys Inn**, which apparently made stockings for Queen Victoria before it became a licensed house.

The centre of the village is a conservation area because of its interesting and largely unspoilt architecture, although most of the outskirts of the village are taken up with new housing for people working in nearby Derby or Nottingham.

The **parish church of All Saints** used to be a chapelry of Elvaston, but became the parish church in 1600. The solid, unbuttressed tower dates from the 13th century, but had its prominent broached spire added later. The chancel is said to have been built by Thomas

Pares, who died in 1805, and his monument is one of a group to members of the Pares family on the south wall of the church. The church was largely rebuilt in the 19th century, when the cast-iron columns were added, together with the west gallery and flat ceiling. The delicate traceried screen was brought here from the Wigston Hospital at Leicester by Thomas Pares, and the Norman font was rescued from the garden of the former rectory and restored to its proper place in 1963.

OLD BRAMPTON (North East Derbyshire)

SK3371: 2 miles (3km) W of Chesterfield

Old Brampton is a charming little stone-built village on the western outskirts of Chesterfield, set among wooded hills on the edge of the Peak District. The three **Linacre Reservoirs,** just to the north of the village, are in the beautiful, wooded surroundings known as Linacre Woods, where there is a popular picnic area and nature trail.

Old Brampton is a one-street village with some fine 18th- and 19th-century houses and cottages, notably Ashgate House, a distinguished Georgian building which is now a hospice. The road leads to the **parish church of St Peter and St Paul**, a mainly 13th- and 14th-century building with a handsome broached spire and some Norman details, such as the south window and doorway. Inside are monuments to Matilda de Caus (1224), slightly obscured, and an ornate Jacobean one to Geoffrey Clarke, who died in 1734. The choir stalls were erected in 1938 to the memory of Thomas Linacre of the nearby

hamlet of Linacre. He was a Fellow of All Souls' and the first president of the Royal College of Physicians. He died in 1524.

On the church's clock face, an amusing detail which few people notice is that when it was installed to mark Queen Victoria's jubilee in 1897, the painter miscalculated and recorded only four minutes between 12 and one, and six minutes between one and two. The local joke is that he had enjoyed too good a lunch in the George and Dragon opposite. Also opposite the church is **Brampton Hall**, a two-gabled, cruck-framed house with mullioned windows, which may have been the ancestral manor house of the de Caus family. The road which leads west over the moors to Baslow, past the Gothic-spired village school built in 1918, is known as Pudding Pie Lane. There is a tiny former Methodist Chapel on the same road which is now a workshop. It was built in 1846 in the grounds of Hollin House.

OSMASTON (Derbyshire Dales)

SK1944: 2 miles (3km) SE of Ashbourne

Mercifully just off the busy A52, Derby-Ashbourne road, Osmaston's story is closely linked with the fortunes of the Wright family, founders of the Butterley Iron Works. It is, in fact, an estate village for the now sadly demolished Osmaston Manor. This splendidly situated, mock-Tudor house was built in 1849 for Francis Wright, owner of the famous ironworks. The house was pulled down in 1964 when the owner at the time, Sir Ian Walker, moved to Okeover Hall near Ashbourne and took the Okeover name. All that survives is the 150ft (45m) tower, cleverly designed to contain all the chimneys for the house – but unfortunately it never worked and more conventional chimneys had to be employed. The Gothic **Park Lodge** still faces the ornamental lake in the lovely grounds, where the former polo field now hosts caravan rallies and the annual Ashbourne Shire Horse Show in August.

The grand, Wright-endowed **St Martin's Parish Church** was built in 1845 to replace an earlier building, and there are many tributes inside to the benefactors. Most of the pretty, brick-built cottages in the village were built by the Wrights to serve their workers, but there are some older houses, a couple of which still stand by the village pond. Many of Osmaston's cottages are still thatched – a real rarity in stony Derbyshire.

OVER HADDON
(Derbyshire Dales)

SK2066: 2 miles (3km) SW of Bakewell

Although Over Haddon is over a mile from Haddon Hall (see BAKEWELL), it gets its name from being the higher of two medieval Haddons – the lower Nether Haddon being a deserted village of which no trace now remains, and which was situated on the hillside above the house and overlooking the Wye Valley. Over Haddon is a typical White Peak village of sturdy, stone-built, mainly 18th century cottages. It stands on the brink of **Lathkill Dale**, one of the loveliest of the Derbyshire dales. The dale was made the first National Nature Reserve in the Peak District in 1972, and now forms the nucleus

of the Derbyshire Dales National Nature Reserve. English Nature has its Peak District headquarters at **Manor Barn** on the edge of the village. At the rear of the headquarters there is an information centre, craft centre and shops. Over Haddon was formerly a centre of the lead mining industry, and there are many reminders of those days in the surrounding fields, and even among the trees in the protected depths of Lathkill Dale. Here the walls of the **Mandale Mine** pump house still stand, ivy-covered now, to remind the walker of how this haven for nature was once a place of industry. The truncated stone pillars of an aqueduct which carried water away from the mine to work a waterwheel can also still be seen in the depths of the dale, and there are also various adits and shafts running off from the daleside path. The Lathkill is one of Derbyshire's disappearing rivers, and in high summer it can often run dry as the water seeps through the limestone. It is also one of the cleanest and purest rivers in the country, unusually running for the whole of its length across limestone. Among the Lathkill's rarities are the pink-flowered shrub, mezereon, and some of the finest stands of the deep-blue-flowered Jacob's Ladder in the country.

Over Haddon was the scene in 1854 of a Derbyshire Klondike and mini-gold rush, after what was thought to be gold was discovered in a lead mine at Manor Farm. A company was formed to extract the ore, and there were even plans to build a railway to Over Haddon from Bakewell two miles away to transport the precious metal away. However, it was eventually discovered that the 'gold' was nothing more than iron pyrites, also known as 'fool's gold', and the enterprise came to nothing. The village pub, the Lathkil (strangely spelt with only one 'l') Hotel, has a good reputation for bar meals and welcomes walkers. **Conksbury Bridge**, to the south-east of the village, crosses the Lathkill by a narrow, low-arched medieval bridge. A possible Iron Age hill fort has recently been discovered above the dale near here.

PARWICH (Derbyshire Dales)

SK1854: 5 miles (8km) N of Ashbourne

Parwich is a pretty limestone village on the edge of the Peak District. It spreads comfortably around its green and village pond (or mere) – once the sheep-wash – above the Bradbourne Brook. It is dominated by **Parwich Hall** (private), a commanding, 18th-century, five-bay house with projecting centre bay and stairs and beautiful terraced gardens on the hill above the village centre. The **parish church of St Peter**, although rebuilt in the late 19th century, still contains much Norman work, including, most significantly, a fine, carved tympanum over the west doorway. This shows the Lamb of God with a cross, a stag trampling on a serpent, a wolf and other strange animals. It was discovered under the plaster. The original Norman chancel arch, with beak heads and grotesques, is now in the tower.

PEAK FOREST (High Peak)

SK1179: 3 miles (5km) E of Whaley Bridge

Once known, because of a quirk of ecclesiastical law, as 'the Gretna Green of the Peak', Peak Forest is a windswept village high on the White Peak plateau, on the A623 east of Whaley Bridge.

The highly unusual dedication of the **parish church of King Charles the Martyr** gives a clue to its extraparochial powers. The original church was built by the wife of the 2nd Earl of Devonshire in 1657, during the time of the Commonwealth's ban on church building – and thus it fell outside the law. The priest, as 'Principal Officer and Judge in Spiritualities in the Peculiar Court of Peak Forest' was able to conduct marriages without question and at any time. The situation continued until early in the 19th century, earning successive incumbents considerable sums of money. Couples can still be married in the church without banns being read, providing that one of the couple has lived in the village for 15 days prior to the ceremony. The present, quite imposing, Victorian church was built on the site of the old chapel in 1878. The Venetian-style window and porch of the old church were reused in the village Reading Room.

The village gets its name because it stood at the centre of the medieval **Royal Forest of the Peak**, not a wooded wilderness in the present sense of the word, but a 40-square-mile (104 sq km) hunting preserve. The Royal Forest of the Peak was a strictly protected habitat of deer, wild boar and wolves which were hunted by kings and princes staying at nearby Peveril Castle at Castleton. In the 16th century, the area surrounding the village was emparked, and managed by a ranger who lived at a house called the Chamber of the Peak, on the site of the present 18th-century Chamber Farm.

About a mile north of the village, on the slopes of Eldon Hill, is **Eldon Hole**, one of the traditional 'Seven Wonders of the Peak' and the biggest open pot-hole in the Peak District. Long thought to be bottomless and an entrance to hell, it was descended for the first time by John Lloyd in 1770 and found to be only 245ft (75m) deep. There are apocryphal tales of a goose being lowered into the awesome void in Tudor times, only to emerge three days later at Peak Cavern, Castleton, with its feathers singed by the fires of hell! Today, the tree-fringed entrance to Eldon Hole is strictly the preserve of expert potholers and cavers.

PENTRICH (Amber Valley)

SK3852: 1 miles (2km) N of Ripley

The 'Pentrich Revolution' may not be as well known as the French Revolution or the English Civil War, but its effect on this small village on the edge of the Pennines was every bit as traumatic. On the night of June 9 1817, a band of between 200 and 300 men led by an unemployed stockinger named **Jeremiah Brandreth**, who styled himself 'the Nottingham Captain', set out towards that city. They threatened to storm its battlements and then, gaining support as they went, march down to London to overthrow the Government and establish a republic. The motley rabble, already disheartened by almost constant rain, was met by a troop of cavalry at Kimberley on the Nottinghamshire border and routed. Three of the ringleaders, including Brandreth, were sentenced to be hanged, drawn and quartered, and fourteen others were transported to Australia.

Those revolutionary times are long gone in today's Pentrich, which is slowly recovering from many years of industrial devastation due to coal mining. In the 1950s, the village took on a derelict air due to mining subsidence, but now it has been revitalised by new housing and the repair of some of the older cottages. The **parish church of St Matthew** is up a steep flight of steps, on a hilltop site overlooking the village, and dates from the late 12th century. It has a fine, pinnacled, Perpendicular-style tower, Norman arcades and an apparently Norman font. Inside there are 17th- and 18th-century monuments to the Horne and Jessop families of Butterley Hall.

PILSLEY (Derbyshire Dales)

SK2471: 2 miles (3km) NW of Bakewell

One of the Chatsworth estate villages, Pilsley is only a mile to the west of the 'big house' and most of the warm, gritstone cottages are still occupied by estate workers. Like those of nearby Edensor, many of the cottages were designed by Joseph Paxton, Chatsworth's head gardener and later designer of London's Crystal Palace. Several of the cottages are much older than those at Edensor and date from the 18th century. Most notable of these is the village pub, almost inevitably named the Devonshire Arms. The village's well-dressings are held in July.

PINXTON (Bolsover)

SK4555: 3 miles (5km) W of Alfreton

Pinxton ware, a very decorative, flower-painted china, is highly collectable. It was made in this former colliery village for a very brief period at the end of the 18th century. William Billingsley, encouraged by the Coke family of nearby Brookhill Hall, on the road to Sutton-in-Ashfield, brought the product here from the porcelain works at Derby, where he had previously worked. It was Billingsley who painted the beautiful flowers which decorated the chinaware. The Pinxton factory was founded in 1795, but it closed in 1812 after he left the business and the quality of the china left with him. The name of China House Square is the only reminder in modern-day Pinxton of its brief moment of ceramic fame.

The red-brick terraces remind the visitor of Pinxton's coal mining past, but the pits are closed now and most residents find work in nearby Mansfield, Nottingham or Derby. The **parish church of St Helen** is mainly a rebuilding of 1750, oddly at right angles to the 13th/14th-century tower and chapel. An aisle and a porch were added in 1939, which gave the church a rather curious and muddled appearance. The painting in the Lady Chapel is attributed to Guido Reni and was given by the Pope to General Coke of Brookhill to the church.

QUARNDON (Amber Valley)

SK3340: 3 miles (5km) NW of Derby

'..a little ragged, but noted village, where there is a famous chalybeat spring, to which abundance of people go in the season to drink the water, as also a cold bath.' Daniel Defoe's description of Quarndon (which he calls 'Quarn' or 'Quarden') in his *Tour through the Whole Island of Great Brit-*

ain, published in 1724-6, recalls the time when this pleasant hilltop village north of Derby threatened to rival Buxton as a health spa. Defoe found the wells 'pretty full of company, the waters good, and very physical, but wretched lodging and entertainment.' Despite that stinging comment, Quarndon spa's distinguished visitors included Admiral Rodley and Dr Samuel Johnson. But Quarndon was never able to realise its potential after an earthquake apparently disturbed the flow of the spring and it dried up altogether in 1897. The only reminders of those exciting days are **Bath Farm**, originally built by the Scarsdale family as an inn in the 18th century but now a hotel, and the little forlorn and embattled Gothic well house near the church. Quarndon later became a centre of the stocking-weaving industry, and some of the older cottages still show signs of their former use with long lines of weavers' windows.

Pevsner dismisses the stone-faced **parish church of St Paul** as 'tasteless and restless', but it has a certain Victorian Gothic charm, with its broach south-west spire.

The Old Father Time weathervane on the pavilion at the village cricket ground in The Common recalls the village's famous victory in the All-England Village Cricket Competition held at Lord's in 1983.

RADBOURNE (South Derbyshire)

SK2836: 4 miles (6km) W of Derby

The pretty village of Radbourne has been the home of the Chandos-Pole family since the 15th century, and the Chandos family had been here since the 13th century, when the little **parish church of St Andrew**, in the grounds of Radbourne Hall, was built. The elegant, red-brick **Radbourne Hall** (private) was built around 1750 by German Pole and probably designed by Francis Smith of Warwick. An open staircase leads up to a Corinthian-columned front door, and inside there is fine rococo plasterwork and marble chimney pieces. Bonnie Prince Charlie is supposed to have lunched with the Pole family in 1745, when his ill-fated uprising reached Derby. The church has a Perpendicular tower, and inside features poppy-headed and traceried medieval bench ends and other woodwork rescued from Dale Abbey. There are many monuments to the Pole family, including an incised slab to Peter de la Pole, dated 1432, and a 1491 alabaster tomb-chest with an effigy of John de la Pole and his wife. The great wall monument to German Pole, erected in 1684, was created and carved by Grinling Gibbons.

REPTON (South Derbyshire)

SK3026: 8 miles (13km) SW of Derby

Repton gives the air of a sleepy little market town, overshadowed by its famous public school. But way back in the seventh century, it was the capital of the powerful Saxon kingdom of Mercia, and the restored, stepped **market cross** in the town centre is said to be the spot where Christianity was first preached in the Midlands.

The slim, elegant 212ft (65m) spire of the **parish church of St Wystan** (a Saxon saint buried here) dominates the town. Its wonderful crypt is one of the most complete Saxon buildings left in the country, and was described by Pevsner as 'a precious survival'. To take the narrow steps down from the transept into the cool, spiral groins of the vault is to be transported back to the days when Penda ruled his kingdom from here, and when the tomb of Wystan was the object of pilgrimage for many. The chancel of the church above still shows the tell-tale, narrow, vertical strips of Saxon work, although the lancet windows above date from the 13th century. The original Saxon church, apart from the crypt, was largely destroyed by Viking raiders, who camped at Repton in 873-74 before moving on to do battle with King Alfred. The nave was added in the 14th century, along with the tower and graceful spire. In 1172, an Augustinian priory was founded at Repton, and a great cruciform church was built to the east of the present parish church. Some foundations of this great priory church survive, with the priory arch and west wing of the cloister court now forming part of the entrance to **Repton School**. The school was founded by Sir John Port of Etwall in 1556. Under the headship of Dr Pears between 1854-74, it grew in fame and reputation, as well as physically. The mock-Tudor **Pears Memorial Hall** was built in his memory by Sir Arthur Bloomfield, and stands on part of the old priory church, its foundations clearly visible. The school chapel was built in 1857, and the theatre to mark the 400th anniversary in 1957. The headmaster's house is known as The Hall and incorporates part of **Priory Overton's Tower**, which was built in the mid-15th cen-

Repton's Market Cross is said to be where Christianity was first preached in the Midlands.

gered European lynx. There are also examples of rare domesticated breeds of livestock as the park is also a Rare Breeds Survival Centre.

Although Smedley built his castle merely as a romantic talking point for visitors to his Hydro in Matlock, after the death of his widow it became a preparatory school until 1929. It was then deserted until it became a Government food store during the war, since when it has been allowed to decay into the gaunt shell seen today.

Although always visible from Matlock, the small hilltop hamlet of Riber is difficult to get to, and has to be approached via Tansley or Cromford. East of the castle stand two charming, 17th-century, mullioned and gabled houses: **Riber Hall**, now an exclusive restaurant, and **Riber Manor House**, which has a date stone of 1633.

tury and is said to be one of the most ornate pieces of early domestic brick architecture in England.

In the town itself, there are many easily recognisable Victorian school buildings, but also many fine 18th-century buildings and one or two half-timbered cottages which may be even earlier. **The Grange** is an early 18th-century brick house, seen though original wrought-iron gates. Easton House is the work of Sir Edwin Lutyens and was built for a housemaster at the school in 1907.

RIBER (Derbyshire Dales)

SK3059: 1 mile (2km) S of Matlock

An eye-catcher for miles around, John Smedley's (see MATLOCK) famous embattled **castle**, built in 1862, is now a roofless shell and the home of the **Riber Castle Wildlife Park**. Here, rare and endangered species are kept and occasionally returned to the wild. The centre has been particularly successful in breeding and returning the endan-

RIPLEY (Amber Valley)

SK3940: 9 miles (14km) N of Derby

Ripley, its large Market Square watched over by a tall, red-brick, 19th-century town hall, prospered as a result of its proximity to the Butterley Iron Works in the early years of the last century. Benjamin Outram (see LITTLE EATON) lived at **Butterley Hall**, on the outskirts of this busy little industrialised town, and the building later became the company's headquarters. Working with his partners, Thomas Jessop and Francis Wright, Outram's ironworks was the first to introduce railway lines into collieries, and in 1868 it also produced the great soaring cast-iron roof of St Pancras Station – the magnificent terminus of the Midland line which greets passengers from Derby and Nottingham. It is claimed that the second syllable of Outram's name – 'tram' – gave the world the name of that particular form of railed transport.

Today, Butterley Hall, with a number of postmodern additions, is the head-quarters of the Derbyshire Police Force.

The **parish church** at Ripley was built in 1820 in the severe 'Commissioners' style, and has an extra wide and very plain interior without aisles, and a plain south-west tower.

RISLEY (Erewash)

SK4635: 7 miles (11km) E of Derby

Mercifully bypassed by the roaring A52 Derby-Nottingham road, Risley is now not much more than a suburb of the latter city, close to Junction 25 of the M1. The two main avenues leading off what was once the main road through this traffic-strangled village are somewhat unimaginatively called First Avenue and Second Avenue. But Risley was first mentioned in the Domesday Book, and **Risley Hall**, opposite the charming and rare Elizabethan **parish church of All Saints**, was once the home of the locally powerful Willoughby family. The present hall (now a private nursing home) was rebuilt in the

early 18th century, and all that is left of the original manor house is the castel-lated balustrade and gateway on the terrace.

The church was built by Michael Willoughby in 1593, but not consecrated until 1632. There is a datestone above the north doorway and a Royal Coat of Arms inside. Michael Willoughby also founded a free school in the village, and another descendant, Elizabeth Grey, built the original Church of England School. The two windmills which once graced the village are long gone, but the road known as Windmill Hill at least recalls one of them.

ROWSLEY (Derbyshire Dales)

SK2566: 4 miles (6km) NW of Matlock

There are actually two Rowsleys – Great and Little. The main village is on the A6 Matlock-Bakewell road, and the minor on the side road to Chatsworth. Travellers on the A6 cannot fail to note Rowsley's most famous building: the beautiful mid-17th-century **Peacock Hotel** in the centre of the village. The bird, which is the badge of the ruling Manners family, is proudly displayed over the pedimented doorway. Originally built in 1652 as dower or manor house for John Stevenson, agent to the Manners family at nearby Haddon Hall, the Peacock to-day is a popular resort of anglers fishing on the Rivers Wye and Derwent. The nearby Grouse and Claret refers to a fishing fly, rather than the game bird and red wine, and is another reference to the piscatorial pursuits of many of Rowsley's visitors. The Grouse and Claret was originally known as the Station Hotel, and it was built after the

The Peacock Hotel, Rowsley

coming of the railway to the village in 1849. Rowsley Station (now demolished), at the back of the Grouse and Claret, was designed by Sir Joseph Paxton as the station for the Duke of Rutland at Haddon. (Not to be upstaged, the Duke of Devonshire's personal station was built at Hassop.) The area of sidings near the station has now been cleared and a new 'leisure village' is under construction. Peak Rail's steam trains now reach Rowsley from Matlock, and there are long-term plans to re-open the line through to Buxton.

The **parish church of St Katherine** dates only from 1855 – until that date, the villagers of Rowsley had to attend either Bakewell or Beeley churches. Inside there is the marble tomb and effigy of Lady Catherine Manners who died in 1859, and her child. There is also a Saxon cross head dating from the ninth century, which was rescued from the river bed.

Just across the road from the church is Caudwell's Mill, a beautifully preserved Victorian corn mill on the Wye, which is thought to be the only water-powered turbine roller flour mill in the country still in operation. There are four floors of fascinating machinery to be inspected, and the visitor can come away with freshly ground flour from the mill. The mill's stableyard is now a craft centre, complete with working demonstrations and a restaurant.

SANDIACRE (Erewash)

SK4736: 7 miles (11km) E of Derby

The Old English name means exactly what it says: 'a sandy piece of cultivated ground'. This hilltop suburban village stands above the Nottingham conurbation, the River Erewash and the constant buzz of the M1. Sandiacre boasts one of the most interesting Norman churches in the county. **St Giles's Parish Church** stands on a rocky eminence, its 13th-century tower high above the rest of the village. The moulded south doorway and aisleless nave, mysterious and dark, all date from the Norman period. But the light and lofty chancel was built by Roger de Norbury, Bishop of Lichfield and Prebend of Sandiacre from 1342 to 1347, and features wonderful traceried windows in the Decorated style, an elaborate canopied sedilia and a piscina. There are memorials to the Charlton family, the earliest of which is to Sir Richard Charlton who died on Bosworth Field in 1485.

SAWLEY (Erewash)

SK4731: 1 mile (2km) S of Long Eaton

Now not much more than a southern extension of Long Eaton, Sawley has been an important terminus for river and canal transport for many years. Standing on the banks of the River Trent and its confluence with the Derwent and Soar, and with the Trent and Mersey Canal running through it, Sawley was ideally placed as an inland port. During the height of its commercial inland waterway fame, so many local people worked on the canals or rivers that they were known as 'Sawley Nosebaggers'. This was a reference to their habit of leaving their donkeys or horses feeding from nosebags while they sought refreshment in local hostelries such as the **Harrington Arms**, a former coaching inn. Sawley is still dependent on its waterside wealth, although now it is leisure boating which is catered for at the enormous **Sawley Marina**, said to be one of the largest in Europe. The marina has in recent years been extended onto flooded land formerly used for gravel extraction. The coming of the marina has seen a welcome revival in the local trade of boat building.

Local tradition has it that the East Midland lace industry was founded in Sawley, and only later spread to Long Eaton and Nottingham. The village specialised in 'flossing' – a type of silk embroidery on lace.

The name of the village comes from the Old English and means 'willow hill'. This refers to the 'sallows' or willows which grew by the River Trent and which were used in basket making. The hill in the village's name is probably the slight rise on which the exceptionally interesting **parish church of All Saints** stands. The chancel roof and arch are of Norman construction, and there is a fine Perpendicular tower and spire and Decorated clerestory. There are medieval monuments and brasses to the local Boothe family, who are thought responsible for the 15th-century tower and spire. But the great glory of All Saints is the late Perpendicular chantry chapel which contains the alabaster effigy and tomb of John Boothe, Treasurer of Lichfield Cathedral, who died in 1496.

SCARCLIFFE (Bolsover)

SK4968: 8 miles (13km) SE of Chesterfield

The legend of Lady Constantia de Frechville, lady of the manor in the late 12th century, is one of Scarcliffe's longest standing legends. Lost with her small child in the forest which then surrounded the village, she heard the curfew bell of Scarcliffe church ringing and made her way towards the sound and safety. In gratitude, she bequeathed land to the church, with the provision that the life-saving bells should be rung three weeks before and three weeks after Christmas for ever after. What is thought to be the tomb of Lady Constantia lies in the nave of the restored Norman **parish church of St Leonard**, whose tower was rebuilt in 1842, when the former spire was removed. The alabaster tomb is unusually large and very beautiful, with the figures supported on a lion. The church has a Norman door, and a Transitional arcade with Early English capitals. The long windows in the nave are of Tudor date, but the beautiful glass of the east window dates from the Victorian restoration.

Unfortunately, the manor house of the de Frechvilles was demolished in 1964, but there are still a number of older cottages in this neat little village, which has managed to retain its traditional rural character despite the industrial scars of the coal mining industry which surround it. Recognition of this admirable fact is that Scarcliffe has regularly featured among the winners of the county's annual 'Best Kept Village' competition.

SHARDLOW (South Derbyshire)

SK4330: 6 miles (10km) SE of Derby

Waterway traffic has been important to this village in the low-lying meadows between the Derwent and the Trent ever since it was first recorded in the Domesday Book of 1086. The original crossing of the Trent was by **Wilden Ferry**, a rope-hauled wooden boat which was replaced by the **Cavendish Bridge** in 1760. This was a toll bridge, and from 1738 part of the Derby-Leicester turnpike. A stone plaque preserved on the approach to the modern (1956) bridge lists the charges which were imposed for the privilege of passing over it. The original Cavendish Bridge collapsed during the bad winter of 1947.

Shardlow is well known to all lovers of Britain's inland waterways as a major stopping off point on the Trent and Mersey Canal, which was built between 1766 and 1777. It has been estimated that the population of Shardlow quadrupled between 1788 and 1841 as a result of the trade brought by the coming of the canal. Although today's trade is almost exclusively leisure boating, many of the warehouses and commercial buildings of the 18th and 19th centuries still line the Canal Bank and The Wharf, which have been protected as a conservation area since 1978. Perhaps the finest of these is stone-faced **Shardlow Hall**, which dates from 1684 and was built by Leonard Fosbrooke, the man behind Shardlow's emergence as an inland port. Other wealthy canal merchants' buildings include Broughton House, on the A6 near the bridge, and the quaintly named Lady in Grey, in Wilne Lane. The **parish church of St James**, opposite Shardlow Hall, dates from 1838, and has unusual cast-iron traceried windows.

SHIRLAND (North East Derbyshire)

SK3958: 2 miles (3km) NW of Alfreton

This quiet little village in the valley of the River Amber has a fine 15th-century **parish church of St Leonard,** with a pinnacled tower and clerestoried nave. There are monuments inside to the Revells of Ogston, who founded a chantry here in the 15th century. There is also a mutilated tomb chest in the north chancel wall which appears to date from the 14th century and may commemorate Sir Henry Grey, who was a member of Parliament in 1377. Ogston Reservoir (see BRACKEN-FIELD) lies to the north, while the small, early 17th-century farmhouse known as Shirland Park, to the south of the village, was originally a hunting lodge.

SMALLEY (Amber Valley)

SK4044: 6 miles (10km) NE of Derby

The village grew up as a clearing in the medieval forest, and was important enough to be recorded in Domesday as having a church, a priest and a mill. Today it stands at the junction of the A608 Derby-Heanor road and the A609 to Belper, and the new housing estates which have spread out from the original village centre generally house Derby commuters.

The **parish church of St John the Baptist** has the distinction of housing in its detached bell tower one of the heaviest chimes of five bells in the country. The bells were the gift of the Revd Charles Kerry in 1912. The church was originally built in 1793, but has been successively Victorianised.

Stainsby House is a large, nine-bay, pedimented, 18th-century, stone house to the south of the village and was built by the Wilmot-Sitwell family, successors to the Sacheverells of Morley.

SMISBY (South Derbyshire)

SK3419: 2 miles (3km) E of Swadlincote

There are many echoes of Sir Walter Scott's *Ivanhoe* in this small, nucleated village which overlooks the Leicestershire plain from the southern spur of Pistern Hill. South of the village, on the road towards Ashby-de-la-Zouch across the border, are the Tournament Fields, marked on the map as 'Manorial Earthworks'. Looking across towards Ashby Castle from the tower of the **parish church of St James**, Scott is said to have been inspired to create his chivalrous medieval romance, and he set the denouement of the drama in the fields below. Many houses, including **Ivanhoe House**, which was originally the posting house inn, have used the Scott connection in their names. Smisby means 'the village of the smiths' and the local story that this was the home of the blacksmiths who repaired the armour of the knights from Ashby Castle could well be true. Ivanhoe or not, the village has a long and distinguished history. Today there would again be trade for a blacksmith, due to the arrival of two racing stables in the village in recent years.

The church contains a weathered alabaster effigy of Joan Comyn, heiress to the lord of the manor who died about 1350. It was through her descendants that the manor came to the Kendall family. William Kendall, who died in 1500, is remembered by an incised slab, and Henry Kendall (died in 1627) is commemorated by an elaborate epitaph with kneeling figures of himself and his wife facing each other across a prayer desk, their sixteen children kneeling below. The linenfold panelling in the east end of the chancel and the tower came from Ashby Castle.

What was the Comyn and Kendall's **Manor House** is the handsome farmhouse (private) next door to the church, but the present building dates only from the 16th century. Another reminder of the old days is the village lock-up, a small octagonal building with a spire and ball on its roof.

SNELSTON (Derbyshire Dales)

SK1543: 3 miles (5km) SW of Ashbourne

This charming little estate village above the River Dove south of Ashbourne could have rivalled Staffordshire's Alton Towers, if Squire John Harrison's plans had been realised. As it was, his enormous Gothic-revival fantasy house of **Snelston Hall**, built to designs by Cottingham in 1827, was modelled on the Earl of Shrewsbury's great pile across the border, and approached it in grandeur. Unfortunately, it was demolished in 1951, but a few embattled walls remain, and the village itself was built in the cottage ornee style by Harrison to match the splendour of his hall. It reminds the visitor of Joseph Paxton's Edensor, near Chatsworth. There is the same mixture of styles, from Flemish brickwork to Gothic-style mullioned windows, and no two seem to be the same. The former inn – the Stanton Arms – is quaintly half-timbered, like the former post office, and retains its heraldic sign of the local Stanton family.

The Perpendicular-towered **parish church of St Peter** dates from the early 19th century and has some colourful late 19th-century glass. The 300-acre (120 ha) park of the hall remains, including some of the monkey puzzle trees which Harrison planted and which were allegedly the first to be successfully grown in Europe.

SOMERSAL HERBERT (Derbyshire Dales)

SK1335: 7 miles (11km) S of Ashbourne

The aristocratic double-barrelled name is a reference to the great FitzHerbert family of Norbury and Tissington. It was they who first held the manor in the 13th century and who built the beautiful, half-timbered **Somersal Hall**, a vision of Elizabethan loveliness described with rare enthusiasm by Pevsner as 'a most felicitous picture'. The house was built by John FitzHerbert and his wife, Ellen, in 1564, as recorded on a wooden tablet just inside the door. The four gables and wealth of patterned timber infillings present a marvellous picture which would seem more at home in Cheshire or Worcestershire than in stone-faced Derbyshire. The south-west block is of brick and was added in 1712.

Next to the hall stands the **parish church of St Peter**, which was rebuilt in 1874, but retained its tub-shaped Norman font, a stained glass window by Kempe, and a monument to the builder of the hall, John FitzHerbert.

SOUTH WINGFIELD (Amber Valley)

SK3755: 2 miles (3km) W of Alfreton

Wingfield Manor (English Heritage), the ruined medieval mansion reached by a farm track half a mile to the south of the village, has the unusual distinction of being built by one Cromwell and destroyed by another. The manor came into the hands of Ralph Lord Cromwell, Lord Treasurer, Warden of Sherwood Forest and Constable of Nottingham Castle, in 1440, and the whole late Gothic building was completed in the short space of twenty years. The house has been described as a second Haddon Hall but, unlike its counterpart near Bakewell, it fell victim to Oliver Cromwell's troops, having changed hands twice in the Civil War. Only the shell of this once magnificent building remains. Earlier, when the manor was in the possession of the sixth Earl of Shrewsbury, it was on three occasions one of the Derbyshire prisons of Mary Queen of Scots. What remains of the manor house is still well worth a visit, especially to see the large Great Hall with its superb vaulted undercroft, the State Apartments, and the 72ft (23m) high High Tower, from which wonderful views can be had down the Amber Valley and towards Crich Stand. Recently these romantic ruins have been used in television and film dramas such as Franco Zeffirelli's *Jane Eyre*.

Some of the missing masonry from the manor found its way to build Wingfield Hall, down the hill from the manor, in 1744. The village of South Wingfield stands at a crossroads on the B5035 Crich-Alfreton road, above the River Amber. It is noted today for the Peacock Hotel, formerly a grange of Darley Abbey, and the local hostelry of the Yew Tree Inn.

The **parish church of All Saints** is some way east of the village, just across the river, and dates mainly from the 13th century. Passing close to the church, the main Midland Line Railway runs through the valley. The former railway station, once described as 'the most perfect of all station houses', was designed by Francis Thompson and allegedly listed Queen Victoria among its stopping passengers.

SPONDON (Erewash)
SK3935: 3 miles (5km) E of Derby

Spondon, now a prosperous suburb to the east of Derby and bisected by the busy A52 Derby-Nottingham dual carriageway, was once a quiet farming village. But the coming of the Industrial Revolution and the phenomenal growth of Derby trebled the population in the 19th century, and it has continued to grow. The Domesday village of Spondon – the name is thought to mean 'the hill where shingle for tiling was obtained' – was virtually destroyed in a disastrous fire in 1340, and the large, spired **parish church of St Werburgh** was rebuilt, along with the rest of the village, during the next fifty years. Unfortunately, Victorian restorers struck in 1826 and 1892, to rob the building of much of its architectural interest.

There are a number of fine Georgian houses in the village centre, the best of which is undoubtedly **The Homestead**, a five-bayed, two and a half storeyed brick house at the top of Willowcroft Road. It was built in 1745 for John Antill, a local tanner, and then passed to Dr James Cade, a Derby surgeon who listed Erasmus Darwin and Joseph Wright, the famous Derby artist, among his acquaintances. His daughter, Rowena, was responsible for building the famous Minack open-air theatre in Cornwall. A later resident was Sir Henry Fowler, chief engineer for the London Midland and Scottish Railway. Two miles to the north of Spondon lies one of Derby's great treasures, **Locko Park**. This splendid open space, centred on an ornamental lake, was once the deer park to the large, early 18th-century, pilastered stone mansion of the same name, the home of the Lowe family. The house was greatly enlarged in the 1850s in the Italianate style, with a tall tower, porch, dining room and picture gallery. In medieval times, the original Locko was a leper hospital for nearby Derby.

STANTON-BY-BRIDGE (South Derbyshire)

SK3627: 6 miles (10km) S of Derby

The 'bridge' in the name is **Swarkestone Bridge** (see SWARKESTONE) across the Trent, and Stanton is the small village on the high ground known as The Hills to the south of the river. One of the three Derbyshire Stantons, (in each case the name appropriately refers to 'stone') Stanton-by-Bridge is perhaps best known for its charming, hilltop **parish church of St Michael**, which has Saxon long-and-short work, a Norman south doorway, west window and chancel arch. Most of the rest dates from the 13th century, apart from the appealing 19th-century bellcot. There is an interesting incised alabaster slab monument to William Sacheverell, who died in 1558, and a recessed effigy of a priest, dating from around 1400. There is a large, brick, Georgian Rectory, and at St Bride's Farm, a mile and a half to the south, a tiny Norman tympanum is preserved.

STANTON-BY-DALE (Erewash)

SK4637: 2 miles (3km) S of Ilkeston

Another **parish church of St Michael** which stands on a hill, in this case overlooking the M1 and the vast, sprawling industrial suburbs of Stapleford and Nottingham. But this little village on Derbyshire's eastern border is surprisingly rural. To the north lies the famous Stanton Ironworks, and for some years during its heyday, only workers from the ironworks were allowed to live in village houses. The church, approached by a line of early 18th-century brick almshouses, dates from the 14th century, but the south doorway has a tympanum with a rude cross, which may be Norman. This pleasant little stone village, with its slim, octagonal cross at the centre, somehow manages to retain its rural atmosphere despite the proximity of so much bustle and industry. Parts of the village were created a conservation area in 1978.

Stanton Hall is a fine 18th-century house with a three-bay centre with rusticated stone lintels on the windows. Stanton's wealth was founded on its quarries, most of which are to the east of the village, near the golf course.

STANTON-IN-THE-PEAK (Derbyshire Dales)

SK2464: 3 miles (5km) SE of Bakewell

The single village street climbs steeply up the western flank of **Stanton Moor**, a strangely isolated, 1000ft (300m) high gritstone outlier in the heart of White Peak limestone country, and one of the richest prehistoric sites in Derbyshire. Over seventy Bronze Age burial mounds have been identified among the heather and birches of the moor, which prompted the historian H.J. Massingham to remark that it was 'as thick with tumuli as a plumduff with raisins'. Among several other ritual monuments on the moor, the most important is the **Nine Ladies Stone Circle and the King Stone** (English Heritage). There are several gritstone quarries, some still active, around the edge of the moor, together with some strange natural formations such as the Andle Stone and the Cork Stone.

The **Earl Grey Tower** is a prominent local landmark on the moor's eastern edge and was erected by the Thornhill family, prominent local landowners, to honour the man responsible for the passing of the Reform Bill in 1832.

Stanton village has some fine 17th- and 18th-century stone cottages, and an inn with the strange name of the Flying Childers – which commemorates the name of a successful racehorse owned by the 4th Duke of Devonshire. Holly House, opposite the pub, still has eight of its fourteen windows blocked, which was done to avoid the Window Tax of 1697.

The initials 'WPT' over the doorways of some cottages stands for William Paul Thornhill of Stanton Hall (private). The hall was the home for generations of Thornhills. The house, behind a high stone wall, has a late 18th-century front backed by a 17th-century rear. The **parish church of Holy Trinity**, dates from 1839 and is unusually aligned from south to north. There is a bronze, Italian holy water stoop, which is dated 1596 and from the workshops of Bellini.

The parish of Stanton also includes the hamlets of Stanton Lees, Pilhough and Congreave, which mainly consist of small farms.

STAVELEY (Chesterfield)
SK4374: 4 miles (6km) NE of Chesterfield

In the heart of industrial north-east Derbyshire, Staveley is dominated by the former ironworks and its railway sidings in the valley of the River Rother. Staveley itself stands to the south, high above the river, and looks down on all this industrial dereliction from higher ground. The large **parish church of St John the Baptist** has a 13th-century tower, the upper parts of which are Perpendicular – as is the south arcade. The church contains some beautiful High Church furnishings, including a rood screen and altar ornaments. Of most interest is the Frecheville Chapel in the south chancel aisle, which dates from 1676. It contains the sad, semi-reclining effigy of Christian Frecheville, who died in childbirth in 1653. She was the daughter of the last Frecheville, later Lord Frecheville of Staveley. Her child, John Pawlet, died a week later and is also buried here. There are other Frecheville monuments in the church, the earliest of which shows Peter Frecheville, who died in 1503, in plate armour.

Staveley Rectory, which later became the council offices, was originally Staveley Hall, and the home of the Frechevilles whose monuments fill the church. The present house was built in 1604, although classically redesigned in the 18th and 19th centuries. Lady Margaret Frecheville founded the Grammar School at nearby Netherthorpe in 1572, and her original gabled building still forms part of Netherthorpe Comprehensive School.

STONEY MIDDLETON
(Derbyshire Dales)

SK2275: 4 miles (6km) N of Bakewell

Stoney by name and stony by nature. Stoney Middleton is squeezed into the narrow valley of Middleton Dale and hemmed in by impending cliffs of limestone and the dusty quarry faces at the western end of the village. It has a long history, which goes back to Roman times. Stoney was on the main highway between the forts at Navio (Brough) and Chesterfield, and although there is no proof of Roman usage, the recently restored **Roman Baths** in The Nook still have the warm springs which may well have attracted the passing legionnaires.

Later the village became a centre for lead mining and lime burning, and old engravings show the dale clear of trees with smoke billowing up from the limekilns.

The **parish church of St Martin**, hidden away off the main street, is one of the most unusual in Derbyshire. An octagonal church, with a lantern roof on piers, was added to the original low, 15th-century Perpendicular tower in 1759. It seems a strange mixture of styles, but it still manages to create a charming impression, with the congregation worshipping 'in the round'. Just to the east of the church is Stoney Middleton Hall, the 17th-century Jacobean former home of Lord Denman, Lord Chief Justice in 1832. Denman was a great Victorian reformer who advocated the abolition of slavery and became the first national chairman of the Women's Institute. He also famously defended Queen Caroline at her trial.

Back on the Main Road, the octago-

'Roman Baths', Stoney Middleton

nal **Toll House** of 1840 now serves as the village 'chippy'. Further along this busy artery is Lover's Leap Café, a favoured resort for rock-climbers who scale Stoney's beetling limestone cliffs. It gets its name from the leap of village girl Hannah Badderley in 1762. Jilted by her lover, she decided to end it all by jumping from the cliff high above the village street. She was saved by her billowing petticoats, which acted as a parachute and deposited her harmlessly on the ground beneath.

Two wells are still dressed every summer.

SUDBURY (Derbyshire Dales)

SK1631: 9 miles (14km) S of Ashbourne

Neat, red-brick Sudbury has a strong claim to be one of the prettiest villages in Derbyshire, and, as often is the case, it owes its perfection to the fact that until fairly recently it was to all intents and purposes a feudal village. The 'big house' in Sudbury's case was the matchless Jacobean perfection of **Sudbury Hall** (National Trust), the home of the powerful Vernon family. The house was started by Mary Vernon in 1613 and completed by her son George between 1670 and 1695. The grand façade by William Wilson has more than a touch of the Baroque which was fashionable at the end of the 17th century, borne out by the hipped roof, balustrade and cupola. Inside, the house has many elegant rooms with plasterwork by Bradbury and Pettifer, painted ceilings by Laguerre and wonderful carved woodwork by Edward Pierce and Grinling Gibbons. The magnificent Long Gallery, reached by a superb carved staircase, fills the whole of the south front of the house. Sudbury Hall was

The Vernon Arms, Sudbury

the home of Queen Adelaide, widow of William IV, for three years after his death. The house is now the home of the National Trust's **Museum of Childhood**, a fascinating insight into how Victorian and Edwardian children worked and played, complete with a genuine Victorian schoolroom, and Betty Cadbury's collection of toys and dolls. In the grounds there is a lovely lake and a strange, castellated Eye Catcher gatehouse folly, built around 1800.

Hidden from view behind the great house stands the **parish church of All Saints**, an over-restored, originally 14th century building with a low tower and many memorials to the Vernons, the earliest of which are the alabaster effigies of John and Mary Vernon (the builder of the hall). There is some fine Victorian stained glass in the east window.

The rest of the village of Sudbury consists of one long street of mainly 17th-century, red-brick and pantiled cottages with the distinguished **Vernon Arms,** built by George Vernon in 1671, at the end. The village was mercifully bypassed by the A50 Derby-Stoke trunk road in 1972, saving it from the worst of the ravages of heavy traffic congestion. HM Open Prison, Sudbury is to the north of the village, near Oaks Green, on a site which was originally an American Army hospital during the Second World War.

SUTTON-ON-THE-HILL (South Derbyshire)

SK2333: 8 miles (13km) W of Derby

The spire of the **parish church of St Michael** is a landmark for miles around and stands half a mile above the small village which it serves, on the gentle hills above the Sutton Brook. The spire was rebuilt on the 14th-century tower in 1831, and most of the rest of the church is of the same date, except for the 14th-century aisle arcade. An unusual wall monument is that of Judith Sleigh who died in 1634. It takes the form of a simple, black, stone coffin, complete with handles, under an elaborate canopy with the coloured arms of the Sleighs. The views from the church are particularly fine, extending to the hills of the White Peak and Tutbury Castle. The 19th-century vicarage later became Sutton Hall and is a distinguished mock-Gothic building with a castellated front.

Sutton was important enough at the time of Domesday to record a church, a priest and a mill. Today it retains its air of detached, peaceful tranquillity, despite the proximity of Derby.

SUTTON SCARSDALE (North East Derbyshire)

SK4468: 4 miles (6km) SE of Chesterfield

The romantic but, sadly, crumbling ruins of **Sutton Scarsdale Hall** are a mute reminder of the lost fortunes of the Leeke family of Scarsdale. The house was built for Nicholas Leeke, 2nd Earl of Scarsdale by Francis Smith of Warwick in 1724, in the grand Baroque style. But by the early 19th century, the Leekes had died out and the house passed to the Arkwright family, hard-headed industrialists who built nearby Arkwright Town. After the First World War, they abandoned the old house, which was threatened by encroaching open-cast coal mining activities. The new owners sold off the best of the classical interiors to the Philadelphia Museum in the USA, where they can still be seen. The house, by now in ruins, was saved from demolition by Sir Osbert Sitwell, who bought it after the Second World War.

Close to the hall is the medieval **parish church of St Mary**, which has a Perpendicular tower and some windows, a porch, chancel and north arcade of the 14th century. There is an incised slab monument to John Foljambe, who died in 1499, and a bust dated 1707 to Samuel Pierrepoint of Oldcotes, or Owlcotes. This is now a farm to the south of the village, but was once the site of one of Bess of Hardwick's great Derbyshire houses.

SWARKESTONE (South Derbyshire)

SK3728: 5 miles (8km) S of Derby

Just over 250 years ago, the three-quarters of a mile (1.2km) long **Swarkstone Bridge**, across the mighty River Trent to the south of Derby, was the scene of one of the momentous incidents in England's history. Here it was in 1745 that Bonnie Prince Charlie's motley rabble of Jacobean rebels turned back from their march on London, little realising the panic their approach had caused in the capital, and that if they had carried on, they would probably have taken the crown and thus changed the face of British history. Swarkstone's most famous monument was originally built in the 13th and 14th centuries and much restored in the early 19th century. Only a handful of arches of Swarkstone Bridge actually cross the Trent, but the long causeway across the low-lying flood meadows of the river are spanned by a further seventeen ribbed arches. The remains of a bridge chapel can still be seen at the northern end of the bridge.

Its strategic position on the northern bank of the Trent has always given Swarkstone an importance which belies its sleepy rural appearance. The oldest monument at Swarkstone is the impressive Bronze Age round barrow cemetery known as **Swarkstone Lowes**, situated on the crest of a ridge overlooking the Trent to the north of the village. Recent archaeological excavations caused by work on the new Derby Southern Bypass have also revealed an Iron Age field system, and a circular timber building which has been dated to the Late Bronze or Early Iron Age in the same area. To the north of the village, on the slopes below Swarkstone Lowes, runs the Trent and Mersey Canal.

Swarkstone Hall, east of the village, was the great house of the Harpurs before they moved to Calke Abbey after the Civil War, when a Royalist force attempting to hold the bridge in 1643 was defeated by Cromwellian Sir John Gell. All that is left of the Harpur's manor is a three-gable fronted house dating from around 1630. The Summer House or Stand is an odd structure near the hall and obviously associated with it, but no one is quite sure what it was used for.

The **parish church of St James** was largely rebuilt in 1876, but the Harpur Chapel contains two alabaster monuments to Richard Harpur (1577) and Sir John Harpur (1627), and a chancel tomb chest to John Rolleston, who died in 1482.

TADDINGTON (Derbyshire Dales)

SK3259: 5 miles (8km) NW of Bakewell

Taddington is a typical, one-street, White Peak village, standing in a little depression at over 1000 feet (300m) above the sea. From Humphrey Gate above the village, fine, sweeping views can be enjoyed down Taddington Dale to flat-topped Fin Cop, and across to the neighbouring hamlet of Priestcliffe.

The close-knit village has regained its rural quiet since the construction of the A6 bypass just after the war. Before that it was on the main road between Bakewell and Buxton, as an iron milestone preserved in the main street recalls. In those days, the Queen's Arms at the eastern end of the village catered for much passing traffic. The Waterloo Hotel, at the other end of the village on the A6, is still a popular hostelry.

The most important building in Taddington is the **parish church of St Michael**, dominated by its slender spire. Dating from the early 14th century, it has an elegant four-bay arcade and a tall chancel lighted by flat-headed windows like those at Tideswell. The church was extensively restored in 1891 and contains a fine brass to Richard Blackwall, his wife and children, which is dated 1505.

Above the village and to the west, on the crest of the escarpment, is the **Five Wells Neolithic Chambered Tomb**, the highest such monument yet discovered in the country. The great limestone slabs of the tomb command a fine view across country to the north. They were originally covered with soil and entered by two low passageways.

TAXAL (High Peak)

SK0079: 1 mile (2km) S of Whaley Bridge

Taxal is a cul-de-sac village overlooking the lovely Goyt Valley on the border with Cheshire, of which it was a part until local government boundary changes of 1936. The chiefly 19th-century **parish church of St James** remains in the Diocese of Chester and the Province of York. It is the fascinating series of memorials which hold most of the interest in the church. In the nave is an inscription to Michael Heathcote 'Gentleman of the Pantry and Yeoman of the Mouth to his late Majesty King George II who died in 1765'. Heathco-

te's duties apparently included tasting the King's food before he ate it as a guard against possible poisoning attempts. There are many other memorials to the Jodrells – a famous Cheshire family now chiefly remembered in many pub names and the Jodrell Bank radio telescope. The earliest is to William Jaudrell 'the Archer' who died in 1375, and Roger Jaudrell, who fought at Agincourt and perhaps was another bowman.

The 17th-century stone-built inn in this tiny village has the unusual name of The Bells of Taxal. Overlooking Taxal to the west are **Windgather Rocks**, an outcrop of gritstone which is a favoured training ground of embryo rock-climbers. To the east stands **Shallcross Hall**, an elegant, early 18th-century, seven-bay Georgian manor house which was formerly owned by the ubiquitous Jodrells and which still has a few Elizabethan windows from the original hall.

THORPE (Derbyshire Dales)

SK1550: 3 miles (5km) NW of Ashbourne

Although Ashbourne calls itself 'the gateway to Dovedale', in reality the tiny limestone village of Thorpe, at the foot of **Thorpe Cloud**, the cone-shaped, rocky, 942ft (287m) eastern portal of the famous dale, has a much stronger claim to the title. It stands near the junction of two of the Peak's prettiest rivers, the Dove and the Manifold, and is the starting point for many enjoyable walks into the heart of these beautiful dales, with the route through Lin Dale to Dovedale's famous Stepping Stones probably the best-known.

Thorpe takes its name from the old

Scandinavian for an outlying farm or hamlet, and after 1000 years, it still has that quality – a remarkable example of the continuity of the Derbyshire landscape. Being the nearest settlement to Dovedale, Thorpe has been in demand for tourist accommodation from the earliest days that 'romantic' scenery became fashionable. Nearest to the village is the large **Peveril of the Peak Hotel**, while at the entrance to the dale, the **Izaak Walton Hotel** recalls the man who first popularised the dale as a place for fishing.

The quaint **parish church of St Leonard** has a stocky little Norman tower and other Norman work inside, together with a fine altar rail which dates from the Elizabethan period. There is a tomb-chest memorial to John Milward, who died in 1632, but it has suffered much damage.

TIBSHELF (Bolsover)

SK4360: 3 miles (5km) NE of Alfreton

The first coal mine to be sunk in Tibshelf was thought to be by Bess of Hardwick, from nearby Hardwick Hall, around the year 1500. But the mines on which Tibshelf's economic wealth was founded for four centuries are all closed now – the last being the Top Pit and Bottom Pit which shut in the 1930s. Many of the old colliery spoil tips and unused railway sidings have now been recovered by nature. The area to the south of the village, where subsidence has created ponds, is now a picnic area and country park, and a popular place for visitors to enjoy the views north to Hardwick across the M1, and west to the hills of the Peak District.

Tibshelf's **parish church of St John the Baptist** stands on a hill near the centre of the village. It is a Victorian creation, the only part of the original medieval building which remains is the Perpendicular tower. There is a small 17th-century brass in the chancel to John Twentiman, vicar of Tibshelf who died in 1683. Newton Old Hall, in the small village to the south of Tibshelf, is a late 17th-century, mullion-windowed manor house, with a fine piered gateway.

TICKNALL (South Derbyshire)

SK3524: 7 miles (11km) S of Derby

The first impressions of Ticknall are all favourable – making it one of the prettiest villages in the county. Surrounded by elegant parklands and well-wooded countryside, Ticknall's red-brick and stone cottages and farms are set haphazardly back from a broad greensward along the long main street, their neat gardens graced by stately pines and quaint roadside water taps. It has all the appearance of an estate village, and the proximity of Calke Abbey proves the point. Many of the houses were built by the Harpur Crewes and their tenants worked on the estate for generations before the houses passed to the National Trust in 1989. The oldest of the houses in the village are probably the **Harpur almshouses**, a long, two-storeyed brick building with a central pediment, which was built by the ruling family in 1772. The circular building with the conical roof, set back from the main street, is the village lock-up, which apparently was still in use for local miscreants as late as 1917.

Ticknall's **parish church of St George** is a simple, Gothic Revival building dating from 1842, but in the churchyard to the south of the present church are the west wall and east window of the original medieval building. This was dedicated to St Thomas à Becket, but was demolished when it became too small for the expanding congregation.

TIDESWELL
(Derbyshire Dales)

SK1575: 6 miles (10km) NW of Bakewell

Tideswell (local nickname 'Tidser') is perhaps best known for its magnificent **parish church of St John the Baptist**, known with some justification as 'the Cathedral of the Peak'. This stately building with its wonderfully light and airy chancel is a rarity among Derbyshire parish churches in that it was almost entirely built within one period – in about 70 years from 1300. This gives the elegant, cruciform building a wonderful uniformity and appearance in the Decorated style, which is missing from so many other churches. Only the pinnacled west tower was added later, in the new and fashionable Perpendicular style. St John's is a delightfully spacious church which contains a wealth of interesting memorials, including some of the finest brasses in the county. Chief among these is the fine one to Bishop Robert Pursglove, who died in 1579, a great benefactor of the village of his birth and the founder of Tideswell's Royal Grammar School (which closed in 1927) in 1560. Earlier fine brasses commemorate Sir John Foljambe (1383) and Sir Robert Lytton, of nearby Litton, who died a hundred years later. Many of the wooden furnishings in the church were carved by the local Hunstone family, who have been woodcarvers of great distinction for three generations.

Tideswell is a large village of ancient

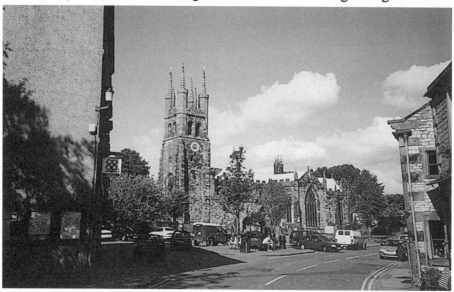

Tideswell Parish Church from the Pot Market

foundation which, like Hartington further south, has the prosperous, urban air of a small town. The present church is on the site of an 11th-century chapelry and the right to hold a market was granted as early as 1251. Edward I stayed at Tideswell for three days in 1275, while hunting in the Royal Forest of the Peak.

At one time Tideswell held five markets a year for cattle and local produce, and those days are recalled in the name of the recently restored, cobbled Pot Market, near the church. Another excellent example of restoration work by the National Park working with the Parish Council is the car park at Cherry Tree Square, at the southern end of the village. Among a range of interesting, mainly 18th-century buildings is The George Hotel near the church, which dates from the latter years of that century and features the Venetian-style shuttered windows which were then fashionable.

The village has a long musical tradition dating back to William Newton (1750-1830), a poet known as 'the Minstrel of the Peak', and Samuel Slack (1737-1822), who sang before King George III. This tradition is continued by the Tideswell Male Voice Choir, the Silver Band, and several smaller choirs.

Tideswell's famous well-dressings are among the finest in the Peak, and take place every year on the patronal festival, or 'Wakes Week', in June. Just to the south of this linear village marked by a fine avenue of beech trees is **Tideswell Dale.** This is a Derbyshire Wildlife Trust Nature Reserve which is noted for its beautiful flowers and exposures of columnar basalt rocks, which make it a geological Site of Special Scientific Interest.

TISSINGTON
(Derbyshire Dales)

SK1752: 3 miles (5km) N of Ashbourne

Neat stone cottages fronting onto broad greenswards, a village green complete with a duck pond (here known as a 'mere'), and everything governed by an elegant Jacobean manor house and watched over by the squat Norman tower of the parish church. For many visitors, Tissington is the complete White Peak village, especially at Ascensiontide when the five beautiful **well-dressings** – traditionally the first, and the earliest recorded in the Peak – are in place. The only thing that Tissington seems to lack is a village pub – for that you have to go to neighbouring Fenny Bentley.

This is FitzHerbert country, and most of the cottages were built and owned by the family which still occupies **Tissington Hall**, as it has for four centuries. Before 1998, the public were only allowed to gaze at this lovely building through Robert Bakewell's wrought-iron gate. But now they are allowed in to see several of the rooms of this charming house, still the home of Sir Richard FitzHerbert and his young family. From the stone-flagged Main Hall, the visitor is shown the oak-panelled Dining Room, dark and mysterious Library and the East and West Drawing Rooms. The present house dates from the early 18th century, but has been much added to over the centuries. It remains one of Derbyshire's

Tissington Hall from the church

most pleasing and intimate manor houses.

Opposite the hall, which has pleasant tea rooms and a restaurant in the former school buildings next door, is the splendid Norman tower of the **parish church of St Mary**. Although heavily restored in 1854, there is still much Norman work to be seen inside, including the south doorway, the chancel arch and the 11th-century tub-shaped font. There is a fine, double-decker, early 17th-century wall monument to Francis FitzHerbert (died 1619) and Sir John FitzHerbert (died 1643) with their wives near the chancel arch, and more family monuments dating from the 17th, 18th and 19th centuries in the chancel.

Avoiding the village in a wide sweep to the east is the **Tissington Trail**, a pleasant walking and riding route which follows the line of the former Ashbourne to Buxton railway line, closed by Dr Beeching's axe in 1967. It was one of the last lines to be built during the 'Railway Age' and opened in 1894. It was re-opened by the National Park Authority as a leisure route in 1971. You can now hire cycles to ride along it, or just enjoy walking along the traffic-free route which passes through some of the finest of the White Peak's rolling countryside.

TRUSLEY (South Derbyshire)

SK2535: 5 miles (8km) W of Derby

The attractive, red-brick **parish church of All Saints**, which was built in the baroque style in 1713, is a charming surprise in this tiny hamlet to the west of Derby. The nave and tower have the fashionable, early 18th-century long-and-short quoin work, and the windows are arched with stone surrounds. The south door is topped by a wonderfully ornate baroque pediment and the interior is almost complete, with box pews, communion rail and an impressive three-decker pulpit. There are many memorials to the Coke family, who first came to Trusley in 1418, but whose original home of Trusley Hall was demolished in the 17th century. All that remains is the part-Elizabethan **Old Hall**, close to the red-brick and gabled Trusley Manor, which was built in 1902.

TUNSTEAD (High Peak)

SK1175: 3 miles (5 km) E of Buxton

The small hamlet of Tunstead lies west of Wormhill, high in the hills above the valley of the River Wye, and is perhaps best known for the massive ICI limestone quarry – one of the largest in Europe – which dominates the west of the settlement. But it was also the birthplace in 1716 of one of Britain's most famous, though unlikely, engineering giants. **James Brindley**, the father of the canal system, was the eldest of seven children of a farmer and moved to Leek in Staffordshire when he was ten. He never learned to read or write, but became an apprentice millwright at 17 and then a millwright in his own right in 1742. His engineering skills brought him to the attention of Francis, Duke of Bridgewater, and it was he who employed Brindley to construct his pioneering Bridgewater Canal to transport coal between Worsley and Manchester. Brindley later constructed many more canals around Britain, and counted Josiah Wedgwood and many other 18th-century worthies among his patrons and friends. He died in 1772 at the age of 56. The cottage where Brindley was born no longer exists, but there is a memorial to Brindley on the village green at Wormhill.

WALTON-ON-TRENT (South Derbyshire)

SK2118: 3 miles (5km) SW of Burton-on-Trent

The great cauldron-like cooling towers of the Drakelow Power Station, standing like a spider at the centre of a web of electricity pylons, dominate the scene to the north of this Trent-side village. But its history long predates these 20th-century monuments to our need for power. To the south of the village, overlooking a bend in the river and its flooded sand pits, is the prehistoric earthwork known as **Borough Hill**, a small hill fort dating from the Iron Age. And above and to the left of the minor road leading to Borough Hill stands Walton Hall, a pleasant, seven-bay, Georgian brick house which was built around 1720 for the Disbrowe family, lords of the manor.

The Norman predecessor of the **parish church of St Laurence**, standing on the northern side of the nucleated village, was mentioned with its priest in the Domesday Book, and there are some Norman remains in the present, mainly 13th-century building. The tower is Perpendicular and the chancery chapel, known as the Waley Chapel, was constructed in 1334 by the rector at the time, Richard Waley, whose mutilated effigy tomb is inside. Another former rector, Thomas Bearcroft who died in 1680, is commemorated by a monument with twisted columns in the chancel.

But most people know Walton for its famous narrow, bouncing **Bailey bridge** linking it with Staffordshire across the Trent. The bridge seems to have been a 19th-century addition. Before that a ferry plied across the river, with the ferryman being supplied from the former Black Swan public house in the village, now replaced by modern housing.

WARDLOW (Derbyshire Dales)

SK1874: 5 miles (8km) NW of Bakewell

The dome-like detached limestone rock known as **Peter's Stone** at the northern end of Cressbrook Dale, to the west of Wardlow, marks the site of Derbyshire's last public gibbeting in 1815. The unfortunate victim was 21-year-old Anthony Lingard, who had been convicted of the murder of Hannah Oliver, the toll-keeper at Wardlow Mires on the main Chesterfield to Chapel-en-le-Frith road (now the A623). William Newton, the famed 'Minstrel of the Peak' was so appalled by the inhumanity of the gibbet that he wrote a poem about it which was to play a large part in the campaign which eventually led to the abolition of the barbarous punishment.

Wardlow itself is a typical one-street limestone village, high on the White Peak plateau. It takes its name from the rounded hill known as Wardlow Hay Cop to the south, and the name is thought to mean 'lookout hill'. The little Gothic-style **parish church of the Good Shepherd** in the main street was built in 1872. Look out for the Victorian letterbox, mounted in the wall near Manor Farm.

WEST HALLAM (Erewash)

SK4341: 2 miles (3km) W of Ilkeston

West Hallam, in the former coalfield country west of Ilkeston, seems a long way from Sheffield's Hallamshire, but the name comes from the Old English and means 'at the nooks of land'. In fact, there are four villages in the vicinity which carry the Hallam suffix: Little Hallam and Hallam Fields have both been swallowed up by Ilkeston, while West and Kirk Hallam, to the west of the town, still have separate identities. Kirk Hallam still retains something of its village character, and clusters around the Victorianised **parish church of All Saints,** which still has some Norman work visible, notably the font. West Hallam is a fast-growing dormitory village for Derby and Nottingham, but there is an industrial estate on what was originally an ordnance depot on Cat and Fiddle Lane, and this provides some employment.

The **parish church of St Wilfrid** dates mainly from the 14th century, and has alabaster memorial effigies to Walter Pontwell (who died in 1598), his wife and children. The war memorial, carved from Sicilian marble, is particularly fine.

Other houses of interest in the village include the **Cinder House** in Station Road, built in 1833 from the cinders made from burnt local clay, and the **Bottle Kiln**, now a buttery and gallery, which stands on the site of the old brickyard, which later became a pottery. The popular annual West Hallam and District Ploughing Match, which originated at the Punch Bowl Inn opposite the church, recalls the village's rural past.

WESTON-ON-TRENT (South Derbyshire)

SK4027: 7 miles (11km) SE of Derby

The small village of Weston-on-Trent

stands high above the river which gave it its name, and looks south across the well-wooded site of **Donington Hall** and its motor racing circuit in neighbouring Leicestershire.

Weston's key position at the highest navigable point on the Trent – reached at King's Mill just across the river – has seen it play an important role in local history. Until the 1940s, the river was crossed by a ferry to King's Mill, but the coming of the Trent and Mersey Canal in the 18th century, took most of the water-borne traffic away from the river.

Buried in the churchyard of the isolated **parish church of St Mary** are two Civil War soldiers allegedly killed in a skirmish at King's Mill in 1642. The 13th-century tower of the distinguished church is said to have been used as a lookout for the approaching army of Bonnie Prince Charlie in his abortive attempt on the British throne in 1745. The church stands some way to the west of the village. A monument in the south aisle commemorates Sir Richard Sale, prebendary of Lichfield Cathedral and a rector here in the 17th century, his wife and children. Also on the outskirts of the village and close to the church is the **Ukrainian Youth Camp**. The Old Rectory also houses a Ukrainian old people's home.

Weston Hall is a large, five-storeyed, Tudor brick building which, unusually for Derbyshire, is moated. It is also claimed to have played a part in the Civil War, when it may have been used for stabling of Cromwell's cavalry. Certainly, the Civil War saw an end to its development as a country house when the owners backed the wrong side.

WHALEY BRIDGE (High Peak)

SK0181: 5 miles (8km) NW of Buxton

The 'bridge' of Whaley Bridge is that which crosses the River Goyt, possibly on the site of a Roman crossing, and this small industrial town has earned the name of 'the gateway to the Goyt'. The beautiful Goyt Valley, flooded by the Errwood and Fernilee Reservoirs, lies just to the south of the town and is very popular with visitors from Manchester and Stockport. Whaley Bridge was transformed by the Industrial Revolution, and the population of what was once an agricultural village had trebled by the mid-19th century. Coal had always been mined in the locality (hence the names Bing Road and Bing Wood, recalling the local name for spoil heaps), but textile mills joined the corn mill on the Goyt. An arm of the Peak Forest Canal was then extended to Whaley Bridge, later to be linked to the Cromford Canal by the Cromford and High Peak Railway – now the High Peak Trail. The steep inclined plane which led down to the canal wharf can still be seen. In 1831, the **Toddbrook Reservoir** was built to the south of the town to act as a feeder for the canal. Nowadays, the canal wharf is busy with colourful narrowboats used for leisure purposes.

In the centre of the bustling little town, the main buildings of interest are the early 19th-century Jodrell Arms Hotel near the railway station, the Wesleyan Chapel (rebuilt in 1867) and Methodist Sunday School of 1821. The **Roosdyche** is a natural feature on the hillside which runs up from the Goyt Valley towards Eccles Pike, to the east of the town. It is a strange, shallow, steep-sided valley about three-quarters of a mile (1.2km) long. For long thought to be a racecourse for Roman chariots, it is now believed to have been a sub-glacial drainage channel dating from the last Ice Age.

WHATSTANDWELL (Amber Valley)

SK3354: 7 miles (11km) S of Matlock

The curious name of this small village on the A6 in the Derwent Valley concerns the ownership of the land at the original crossing of the river in 1390. The ford was next to the house of Walter (or 'Wat') Stonewell, hence 'Watstonewell', and was known as 'Wattestanwell Ford'. Wat entered into an agreement with the Abbot of Darley and John de Stepul, who intended building the first bridge on the site. Next door to the modern bridge is the ivy-clad **Derwent Hotel**, a popular eating house and formerly a coaching inn known as the Bull's Head. The scattered village shares Crich's parish church, and the Methodist Chapel, built in 1877, closed in 1988. Florence Nightingale used to alight at Whatstandwell Station on the last leg of her journey home to Holloway.

WHESTON (Derbyshire Dales)

SK1376: 5 miles (8km) E of Buxton

The great glory of Wheston, a tiny farming hamlet near Tideswell, is its almost complete 15th-century village cross, one of the best in the county and a scheduled ancient monument. It stands some 12ft (3.6m) high on four steps inside a walled enclosure surrounded by trees, and features a cusped head and a rather primitive carving of the Crucifixion and the Virgin Mary. **Wheston Hall** (private) is a charming Georgian manor house which probably stands on the site of a much older house.

WHITTINGTON (Chesterfield)

SK3975: 2 miles (3km) NE of Chesterfield

The twin villages of Whittington, Old and New, are now submerged into the northern suburbs of Chesterfield. Old Whittington lays claim to being the birthplace of the 'Glorious Revolution' which brought William of Orange to the English throne in 1688. It was here, in what is now known as the **Revolution House**, but which was then the Cock and Pynot (a local name for a magpie) Inn, that the first Duke of Devonshire and other noblemen plotted the downfall of James II and the eventual coronation of William III and Mary II in 1689. The old thatched house, at the junction of the old Sheffield and Rotherham road, is now a museum furnished in 17th-century style which tells the story of those fateful days at the end of that turbulent century. A modern **Cock and Magpie** Inn still stands nearby.

Today, Whittington is a pleasant suburb of Chesterfield, but in the early 18th century it was an industrial centre famous for its glassmaking, recalled by the name of Glass House Common. Richard Dixon made a variety of plain and coloured drinking glasses as well as bottles for wine, sack and ale. It was the Dixon family who built Whittington Hall in the 19th century, now a centre for mentally disabled people. The parish church of St Bartholomew was built in 1896 to replace a church which was destroyed by fire a year before. This earlier church was itself on the site of a Norman building. New Whittington's **parish church of St Barnabas** is a more modern affair, dating from 1927.

WHITWELL (Bolsover)

SK5276: 10 miles (16km) E of Chesterfield

Although surrounded on all sides by the remains of industry, the former coal mining village of Whitwell in northeast Derbyshire retains its rural atmosphere and is blessed with two of the finest Norman churches in the county. Standing at the gates of Welbeck Abbey, just across the border in Nottinghamshire, Whitwell was mentioned as early as 942 in the *Anglo Saxon Chronicles* as 'Hwitan wylles geat' – which translates as 'the clear spring or stream in the valley'. This probably refers to the stream locally known as 'The Dosh', which runs through the planned woodland of Whitwell Wood. The wood was laid out in the style of the Forest of Versailles by the Duke of Portland from nearby Welbeck. The woods can still be enjoyed via a series of waymarked forest walks.

There is still a well complete with pump in the village square, and another on the village green which supplied the whole village with drinking water until mains water was laid.

The **parish church of St Lawrence** is of unusual size and magnificence. Dating from Norman times are the tower, the nave with its rare, untouched clerestory, and a superb west arch, once described as one of the most perfect Norman arches in the country. The chancel and transepts are in the Decorated style. Built in the first half of the 14th century, they feature some beautiful traceried windows. To top all this there is Jacobean panelling in the chancel, and a wall monument to Sir Roger Manners, son of Dorothy Vernon of Haddon Hall, who died in 1632. Manners lived at the 17th-century gabled Manor House just north of the church, which with the rectory designed by J.L. Pearson provides a perfect picture.

To the south of the village lies the enormous **Steetley Quarry**, from which Dolomitic limestone is extracted to line blast furnaces. The quarry takes its name from the tiny hamlet of Steetley, on a minor road two miles (3km) to the north-east, where the original limestone quarry was sunk.

But Steetley's great secret is its perfect little Norman **chapel**, embowered by trees and described by Pevsner as 'by far the richest example of Norman architecture in Derbyshire'. No one knows why such a little gem of 12th-century Decorated architecture was built here, or how it managed to survive almost untouched until today. The 1880 restoration, which replaced the missing roof of the nave and some of the decoration, was for once tastefully carried out by the same J.L. Pearson who built Whitwell Rectory. The chapel, astonishingly, dates from the time of King Stephen (1135-54), and consists of a nave and chancel which end in a semi-circular apse. The whole building measures only 56ft by 15ft (17m by 4.5m), but it is richly decorated with medallions, foliage scrolls, zigzag mouldings and weird and wonderful animals, such as a double-headed lion and St George and the Dragon. 'There are few Norman churches in England so consistently made into show-pieces by those who designed them,' says Pevsner.

WILLINGTON (South Derbyshire)

SK2928: 6 miles (10km) SW of Derby

Situated close to the great new under and overpasses of the junction of the A50 and A38 south of Derby, Willington has been at the hub of transportation for over two centuries. The River Trent passes to the south, and the Trent and Mersey Canal follows the line of the Midland Railway through the village. But Willington's position on the gravels of the northern bank of the Trent was important long before the Transport Revolution put it on the map. Archaeologists have made several discoveries of artefacts dating back to the Bronze Age and Roman times in the gravel beds by the river. These are now in the Derby Museum. The A38 follows the line of the Roman Ryknield Street between Lichfield and Derby.

Today Willington is overshadowed by the great cooling towers of the power station to the north of the village, one of several built in the 1950s in the broad flood plain of the River Trent.

The **parish church of St Michael** retains a damaged Norman tympanum over its south door, but most of the rest dates from the early years of the 19th century, when it was heavily restored. It enjoys fine views across the River Trent towards the spire of Repton church from its modest tower.

WINGERWORTH (North East Derbyshire)

SK3867: 3 miles (5km) S of Chesterfield

Wingerworth has stoutly resisted becoming a suburb of Chesterfield, and retains its own identity, surrounded by well-wooded countryside which was once the deer park of the Hunloke family of the demolished Wingerworth Old Hall. A long-standing tradition about this staunch Roman Catholic family concerns Sir Thomas Hunloke, who died in 1816. He invited French prisoners of war held at Chesterfield to attend mass in the Roman Catholic chapel of the hall. But the prisoners were not allowed to go further than a mile from Chesterfield – so they are supposed to have uprooted the tell-tale milestone on the road from the town and carried it with them to Wingerworth. The original hall was built in 1590 by Sir Henry Hunloke and later rebuilt by Francis Smith of Warwick for the third baronet. The first baron had been knighted by Charles I on the first battlefield of the Civil War, at Edge Hill in 1642. When the baronetcy died out in 1856, the estate was sold and the hall demolished, leaving only the north and south wings near the **parish church of All Saints**. This too has undergone a transformation, with a new church being built onto the north side of the original Norman building. The old church retains a rare medieval rood loft and the 13th-century effigy of a priest. There are many memorials to the Hunloke family.

The proximity of the north Derbyshire coalfield has meant that Wingerworth has suffered its share of industrialisation, and the site of the former Avenue Colliery, east of the A61 Derby road, is now a smokeless fuel plant, opened in 1956. Stubbing Court, now a farm, is a seven-bay, pedimented stone house dating from around 1700. It is situated in parkland in the fields to the west of Wingerworth.

WINSTER (Derbyshire Dales)

SK2460: 4 miles (6km) W of Matlock

Winster is one of Derbyshire's most complete 18th-century villages and, like Bakewell and Hartington, it gives more of an impression of a small town. But it was not granted the right to hold a market until around the turn of the 17th century, and the grand **Old Market Hall** (National Trust) dates from the end of that century. Like Bakewell's Market Hall, it originally had an open ground floor with pointed arches, to which was added a brick upper floor and gables. The arches are now filled with brick, and the building became the first National Trust property in Derbyshire and the Peak District in 1906. Pilastered Winster Hall, almost opposite, was the 18th-century Georgian-style home of Llewellyn Jewitt, the distinguished late 19th-century Derbyshire antiquarian, and is now a public house. The inn sign of Winster Hall shows the famous Winster Morris Men, one of the oldest troupes in the country, who have their own dance and tune and who remain very popular at local festivities. Another famous Winster tradition is the Pancake Race held annually on Shrove Tuesday.

The Old Market Hall, Winster

The double-gabled **Dower House** at the western end of Winster's main street has a 17th-century date, but most of Winster's street of fine houses date from the 18th-century heyday of the local lead mining industry. This is also reflected in the name of the Miner's Standard Inn, just outside the village at the top of West Bank, which recalls the unit of measurement of lead ore.

The **parish church of St John the Baptist** has an unusual two-aisled nave which was added in 1833 and which is divided by a lofty arcade. The rather plain tower dates from 1721.

WIRKSWORTH (Derbyshire Dales)

SK2854: 3 miles (5km) S of Matlock

Wirksworth, hemmed in by limestone quarries and founded on the wealth

The Moot Hall: home of the lead miners' Barmot Court in Wirksworth

won from lead mining, is a town founded on its mineral wealth. But when the lead mining industry collapsed in the 19th century, Wirksworth became a sad place. The shops and businesses in its steeply sloping, cobbled Market Place became run down and many closed. It is to the credit of the local Civic Society, the Civic Trust and the Derbyshire Historic Buildings Trust among others that the town underwent a marvellous transformation in the 1980s, winning several awards for the restoration of the town centre. Today, Wirksworth – the 'Snowfield' of George Eliot's *Adam Bede* – is a tourist centre in its own right, with many places of interest to show the discerning visitor. Chief among these is the **parish church of St Mary**, which stands in what is almost a cathedral-type close just off the Market Place. And among St Mary's greatest treasures is a Saxon coffin lid, only discovered in 1820, which must have been from the sarcophagus of a very important person. It

is probably the earliest Christian monument in the Peak, and dates from around 800. It is embellished with vigorous carvings which show scenes from the life of Christ, including about forty stumpy figures which show the washing of the disciples' feet, the burial of Christ, his descent into hell and ascension, among others. There are numerous other Norman architectural fragments in the north transept of the church, plus a Norman font. The architecture of the cruciform church itself compares with Ashbourne in grandeur. Although heavily restored by Sir George Gilbert Scott in 1876, it dates originally from the 13th and 14th centuries, with a crossing tower, transepts and aisled chancel. There are 16th-century monuments to the Blackwell and Gell families, including a fine alabaster effigy of Anthony Gell, the founder of Wirksworth's major school, who died in 1583, and the celebrated Parliamentarian General, Sir John Gell.

Also in the Church Close are the 15th- and 16th-century **Priest's House, Gell's Almshouses** built in 1584, and the Gell's original **grammar school**, founded in the same year, but rebuilt in the Gothic style in 1828. There are a number of other mainly 18th-century stone houses in the town centre, including the Old Manor House which is a Georgianised early 17th-century house, and the mid-Georgian Red Lion Inn. On the outskirts of the town centre is the Tudor Old Hospital, a gabled building of 1588.

The **Moot Hall** in Chapel Lane is the place where the lead miners' Barmoot Court still meets twice a year to settle the disputes, which today are very rare. It is a plain, one-storey building which was rebuilt in 1812. A miner's arms, scales, pick and trough are carved on the front. Inside, the bronze standard measuring dish for lead ore (14 pints) which was made in 1512 still hangs on the wall of the courtroom.

Wirksworth holds its **well-dressings** on the late Spring Bank Holiday, and still conducts the annual ceremony of Church Clypping – or embracing the church boundaries – in September.

WORMHILL (High Peak)

SK1274: 4 miles (6km) E of Buxton

The ornate memorial to James Brindley, who was born at nearby Tunstead (see TUNSTEAD), was erected on the pretty, sloping village green at Wormhill in 1895, and now serves as the centrepiece for the village **well-dressings** in August.

Wormhill's little **parish church of St Margaret** has an unusual Rhenish helm-type tower, similar to the Saxon one at Sompting in Sussex. It was largely rebuilt in 1864 on a medieval tower. **Wormhill Hall** (private) is an attractive, H-shaped, late 17th-century stone mansion on the approach to the village from the Wye valley. It was built by the local Bagshawe family in 1697. **Old Hall Farm**, north of the village centre, dates from the 16th and 17th centuries, and may have been the original Manor House for Wormhill before the hall was built.

YEAVELEY (Derbyshire Dales)

SK1840: 4 miles (6km) S of Ashbourne

Yeaveley is one of those south Derbyshire villages stranded in a time warp in the rolling, largely forgotten countryside south of Ashbourne. It was the birthplace of one of the greatest architects of the Middle Ages, **Henry Yevele**, who was thought to be responsible for the rebuilding of the great naves of Westminster Abbey and Canterbury Cathedral. The small, red-brick **parish church of Holy Trinity** in the village centre was built in 1840. The original manor house of Yeaveley was **Stydd Hall**, now nothing more than a farmhouse a mile to the west of the village, and reached down an unmetalled, private road. The hall features the remains of a preceptory of the Knights Hospitallers, founded in 1190. One wall of the 13th-century chapel remains, with lancet windows. The present brick and stone farmhouse stands on these medieval stone foundations, but is chiefly Elizabethan or Jacobean in date. Another link with the medieval past lies to the south of the village in the valley of the Bentley Brook, where bumps and hollows mark the site of the deserted medieval village of **Hungry Bentley** – perhaps a significant name – near the Bentley Fields Open Farm.

YOULGREAVE
(Derbyshire Dales)
SK2164: 2 miles (3km) S of Bakewell

A word must be said first about the name of this charming, one-street, ridgetop village above Bradford Dale. According to one source, there have been more than sixty different spellings of its name, and even today, there is controversy. Locals all spell it 'Youlgrave', which is how it is pronounced, but the Ordnance Survey and various other branches of officialdom insist on inserting the extra 'e' to call it Youlgreave. The name is thought to mean 'yellow grove' or 'the grove of Geola' – a 'groove' being the old term for a lead mine, an important industry in these parts for at least 200 years. In common with many other larger Peak District villages, Youlgreave has its own local nickname, in this case 'Pommy'. It is thought to relate to the sound made by a local pig leaning over a wall and hearing the 'tiddley pom, pom, pom' of the village silver band, but no-one will swear to it!

The first thing the visitor notices about Youlgreave is the magnificent Perpendicular pinnacled tower of the **parish church of All Saints**, widely regarded as one of the finest in Derbyshire. Inside, the impressive south arcade is late Norman in date, later extended to the west without aisles – the whole crowned by a clerestory. The splendid chancel is graced by some fine monuments, the best of which is in the centre and is a charming, miniature alabaster effigy of the armoured Thomas Cockayne, who died in 1488. His head rests on a cockerel, an amusing pun on the family name. In the north wall is the early 14th-century cross-legged effigy of a bearded knight holding his heart in his hands. Other monuments in this fascinating building include a beautiful oblong panel to Robert Gylbert who died in 1492, his wife and their seventeen children. On the north wall, opposite the entrance, is a delightful cameo of a little stone pilgrim carrying her staff and bag. The east window and the south window in the chancel are both among Edward Burne-Jones's stained-glass masterpieces, and there are others by Kempe in the north aisle and south nave.

Just down the main village street – known as 'Derbyshire's longest car park' – is **The Fountain**, the circular water storage tank built in 1829 for the village's own private water supply. Unusually, Youlgreave still has its own water supply company.

Opposite the Fountain is **Youlgreave Youth Hostel**, formerly the village Co-operative Society stores and built in 1887. It retains the names of the departments on its dormitory doors, so that male visitors can claim with impunity that they slept in 'Ladies Underwear'. Further down the village street is the **Old Hall**, a mullion-windowed and gabled building which dates from 1650. Behind it and unseen from the street is **Old Hall Farm**, which is even older, dating from 1630.

Youlgreave's celebrated **well-dressings** date from the setting-up of the Fountain in 1829, and are among the most accomplished and widely admired in Derbyshire.

Select Bibliography

Barnatt, John and Smith, Ken, *Peak District: Landscapes through time* (Batsford/English Heritage, 1997)

Cameron, Kenneth, *The Place-names of Derbyshire* – three volumes (Cambridge University Press, 1959)

Cooper, Brian, *Transformation of a Valley: the Derbyshire Derwent* (Heineman, 1983)

Mee, Arthur, *Derbyshire* (Hodder & Stoughton, 1937)

Millward, Roy and Robinson, Adrian, *The Peak District* (Eyre Methuen, 1975)

Pevsner, Nikolaus,*The Buidings of England: Derbyshire* (Penguin, 1953)

Smith, Roland, *First and Last* (Peak Park Joint Planning Board, 1978)

Smith, Roland, *The Peak National Park: Official Guide* (Webb & Bower/Michael Joseph, 1987)

Thorold, Henry, *Shell Guide to Derbyshire* (Faber & Faber, 1972)

Various authors, *Peak District Leisure Guide* (AA/Ordnance Survey, 1987)

Various authors, *The Derbyshire Village Book* (Countryside Books/Derbyshire Federation of Women's Institutes, 1991)

Index

Also of interest from:

PEAK DISTRICT MEMORIES: the photographs of E. Hector Kyme

After the photographer Hector's Kyne's death, Roger Redfern, well-known writer and long-time friend, was granted permission to select photographs representative of Kyne's great talent from the last thirty years of his life. The result: a visual celebration of the changing moods and scenery of the Peak District which would be a valuable addition to the bookshelves of all ramblers and other lovers of England's wild places.

£9.95

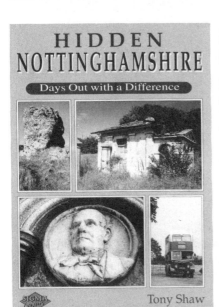

HIDDEN NOTTINGHAMSHIRE – Days Out With A Difference

Local historian and amateur archaeologist Tony Shaw has turned his attention to Nottinghamshire in this fascinating new book. Both county residents and tourists will now be able to discover 100 places of interest which do not feature in any other guidebook: a tiny Robin Hood theatre, a holy well, King John's hunting lodge and hexagonal toll-house. You'll be amazed at what Nottinghamshire has been hiding from you for so long!

£6.95

TEA SHOP WALKS IN THE PEAK DISTRICT

At the end of a walk in the Derbyshire Peak District, treat yourself to a tried and tested tea shop. The walks are all easy-going and highly suitable for family groups. There are several more "Tea Shop Walks" from the popular walking duo Norman and June Buckley, who are quickly becoming the country's tea shop experts - "...the shape of things to come...highly recommended" THE CONGLETON CHRONICLE

£6.95

WALKING THE PEAK DISTRICT DALES

Circular, flexible walks for all - but much more than a simple walking guide. Chris Holmes conveys a fresh view of the White Peak, challenging accepted historical truths and questioning current views on tourism. His inspirational book encourages "an individual response to the White Peak".

£6.95

All of our books are available through your local bookseller. In case of difficulty, or for a free catalogue, please contact:
SIGMA LEISURE, 1 SOUTH OAK LANE, WILMSLOW, CHESHIRE SK9 6AR.
Phone: 01625-531035; Fax: 01625-536800.
E-mail: sigma.press@zetnet.co.uk . Web site: http//www.sigmapress.co.uk

VISA and MASTERCARD welcome. Please add £2 p&p to all orders.